D0516742

A Taste of Mexico

Vegetarian Cuisine

Kippy Nigh

Book Publishing Company
Summertown, Tennessee

© 1996 Kippy Nigh
Cover Design: Jeffrey Clark
Cover Art: Nina Diakova
Illustrations: Kippy Nigh, Otis Maly (pages 46, 83)
Interior Design: Cynthia Holzapfel, Michael Cook
Back Cover Photograph: Craig Dietz

The Book Publishing Company
PO Box 99
Summertown, TN 38483

02 01 00 99 98   6 5 4 3 2

ISBN 1-57067-028-5

All rights reserved. No portion of this book may be reproduced by any means whatsoever
except for brief quotations in reviews, without written permission from the publisher.

Nigh, Kippy
    A taste of Mexico : vegetarian cuisine / Kippy Nigh,
        p. cm.
    Includes Index
    ISBN 1-57067-28-5 (alk. paper)
    1. Vegetarian cookery. 2. Cookery, Mexican. I. Title.
TX837.N55 1996
    641.5'636'0972--dc20   96-30625
                                                                          CIP

Dedication
To the unlimited happiness of everyone who loves to cook, of
everyone who loves to eat, and everyone who loves.

Calculations for the nutritional analyses in this book are based on the average number of servings listed with the recipes and the average amount of an ingredient if a range is called for. Calculations are
rounded up to the nearest gram. If two options for an ingredient are listed, the first one is used. Not
included are fat used for frying, unless the amount is specified in the recipe, optional ingredients, or
serving suggestions.

Contents

The Story Behind the Cover

When Nina Diakova appeared in La Casa del Pan and asked me if she could stay at our house, it was Christmas Eve, 1993. She came to me at the suggestion of our mutual friend and painter, Jose Monjarraz. I told her the house was full, with our three children and their closest friends camping out in the living room and my husband and I occupying the only bedroom, and that she would probably be more comfortable in one of the local inns. She told me that all the inns and hotels were full. At that point my daughter Amy told me we should definitely take her in, even if only on the shared floor. The Russian people had been so kind to her and her three friends when they visited Russia the year before, putting them up on the floors of their tiny apartments. So we welcomed her to join us and shared a memorable Christmas Eve dinner together. My kids picked out some amber earrings to give her, so she wouldn't feel left out. She was very discreet and helpful, and we shared our life stories in Spanish, since she didn't speak English. We told her she was welcome to stay as long as she liked, for which she was very grateful, since she had very little money and was eager to paint watercolors of San Cristobal, where the light is very beautiful and the colors shine.

Nina painted every day and she gave me some instruction as well. Then came New Year's Eve. We had a dinner party at La Casa del Pan with family, staff, and clients, dancing until 3 a.m., with the doors wide open to the street. At around 4 a.m., we crashed into our beds. I bounced right back out of bed at 5 to take our son Ian to the airport so he could return to school in Massachusetts. On the way through town, we noticed groups of soldiers standing on the street corners, and I commented to Ian on it. "They must be here because of all the New Year's Eve celebrations," he suggested. "Yeah, maybe so," I remarked, "but this is very unusual. There are really a lot of them." We drove on to the highway, where we saw a group of about thirty soldiers standing by the road. "Something has definitely happened. Look at all of them here," I told my son. "Hmmm, maybe so, Mom, but we've gotta keep going. I *have* to be back at school tomorrow." (This, coming from a boy of seventeen? Well, really, his girlfriend there was the reason.) So we kept going.

The next thing we saw was a group of tourists strung out along the highway, bags in hand, walking toward San Cristobal. Their leader, a local guide, waved emphatically for us to stop. We asked him what was going on. He said, "There are hundreds of armed Indians up ahead. They've blocked the highway and they've taken our bus. Don't go there or they might take your car." "Who are they?" I asked him. "They're from around Ocosingo. They've finally revolted. It's a revolution!!!"

We gave him a ride to the center of town, where it was now 5:30 a.m. As we approached the municipal government building, the soldiers stationed all around it trained their rifles on our car, and the foremost among them motioned for us to take the long way around, which we did. We left the guide at his destination and returned home, much to Ian's frustration. I woke his father with the statement, "The revolution has started. The highway to Tuxtla is blocked by hundreds of armed Indians. They have an army and have taken the town."

It took about three long minutes for that to sink into his dream state, but when it did, he sat up, unbelieving but interested. So began a new chapter in the history of the Chiapas highlands, a place of surreal people and happenings.

So what does that have to do with the cover? Nina went out as soon as she could, to paint La Casa del Pan in the crystal clear light of January 1st, 1994.

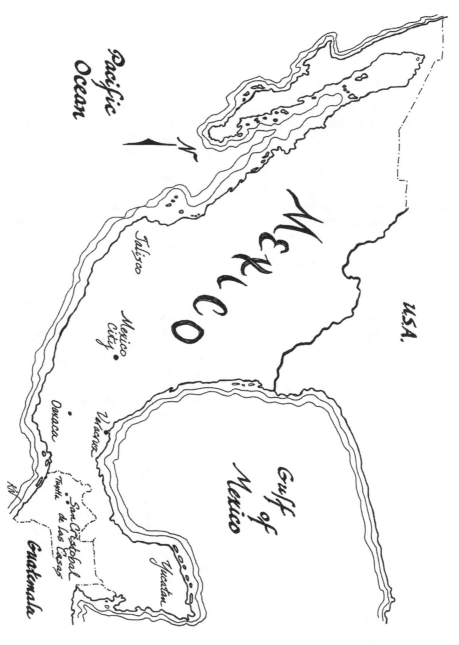

Pacific
Ocean

Mexico

U.S.A.

Jalisco

Mexico
City •

Oaxaca •

Veracruz

Gulf
of
Mexico

San Cristóbal
de las Casas

Yucatan

Guatemala

Map 5

Acknowledgments

I can't say these recipes are mine. I can't even say they belong to those people who have fed me bounteously over the years. They come from a vast pool of the human spirit: generations of humanity sharing food and recipes with an open heart, adapting them to their needs. My contribution has been to work on them, transform them to meet my standards of nutrition and taste, serve them in our restaurant, and pass them on to you.

I want to thank the vibrant and loving people of Mexico for showing me the joys of Mexican cuisine, from the reverent growing of organically-produced food, to its artistic preparation, to the celebration of eating among loved ones. My husband Ron has contributed a number of these recipes, and polished many others. After my mother, he was the person who most guided me towards good cooking, being a very appreciative diner and enthusiastic cook. The combination of my mother's generous, nutritional approach to cooking and Ron's efficient, ecological, ethnic orientation laid the foundation for the philosophy which is the core of this work. I thank them both with all my heart. They taught me how to make cooking an expression of love.

I also thank my friends Margarita Sires, Maria Luisa Lignarolo, Barbara Torres, Bertha Barraldi, Alicia Michel, Alicia Rosado, Jodie Randall, Carmen Ramirez, Beatrice Uribe, Marcey Jacobson, Janet Marin, Mimi and Bob Laughlin, George and Jane Collier, John and Lourdes Haviland, María Elenna Fernandez, Kees Grootenboer, Angela Cuevas, Andrés Aubrí, Kiki and Gabriel Suarez, Carol Kurasik, Virginia Sanchez Navarro, Carol MacQuire, June Nash, Carlota Duarte, Leslie Devereaux, Rama and Marguerite Elliott, Flora Edwards, Jane Taylor, John and Julie Haehl, Cristine, Ted and Carmen Downing, Susanne Jaqueline, Sandra Blakeslee, Betty and John Thompson, Bob Hubbard, and Betsy and Pogo Blackmer, who have all contributed to this book by sharing food and recipes, as well as their friendship, with me. There are many others, as well, too numerous to name here but well-remembered.

I give special thanks to my friend and administrator, Marta Zarate, for her loyal support through thick and thin, also to my soul sister Flor de María Navarro, who cared for me every day, and to Gilberto de la Cruz, who, as manager, gave his heart and transformed La Casa del Pan and me. I thank my student, head baker, and friend Jero for his unfailing help and friendship. And I thank Dona Mari, who taught me traditional Nahuatl recipes and helped me in the kitchen for as many years as she was able. Thanks also to Florenica, Gregoria, and Aurelia who shared their Oaxacan flavors with me. Thanks to Dan Komer, a big heart in the kitchen and our much-loved neighbor. Thanks to Jim and Mary Nations. Thanks to the Musi family: Jorge, Julia, Vanessa, and Jenny, also Carlos and Josefína, all of them cooking geniuses with flare. Thanks to Maria Luisa Porras, who taught me my first Spanish years ago, as she showed me San Cristobal cuisine and talked witchcraft and her philosophy of life. Thanks to Cristina for years of laughing while I practiced perfecting my tortilla technique with her over an open fire . Thanks also to Manuela, who cheerfully accompanied me to market many times and made many of these recipes with me. Special thanks to Raymunda Bermudez and Juan Diego Lunes; they were the first helpers to answer my ad in San Cristobal. They either arrive for work before dawn or stay until the wee hours of the morning, if necessary, and do it with good humor. Special thanks to Celia García Ballinas, who began as a dishwasher and gradually learned to be an expert cook and who good-naturedly directed the morning kitchen at La Casa del Pan. Thanks to Paula for teaching me how to wait tables and make the first menu. Thanks to Gita. Thanks to Don Jeronimo, Mario, Cata, Jose Luis, Geno, Manuel, Israel, Rosalva, Elena, Jenny, Irma, Mari, Gerardo, Raul, Federico, Rosi, Carolina, Laura, Beti, Jorge, Eliseo and others, for helping, at one time or another, in La Casa del Pan in Mexico City or in San Cristobal. I couldn't have done it alone. Thanks to Tona and Maruch and Rosalina and Marcelina and their numerous sisters, who taught me many skills, including how to make tortillas and beans and carry water in an earthenware pot on my back up a muddy trail. Thanks to Ambar Past for her Tzotzil cookbook and her poetry.

Heartfelt thanks to Amy, Alina, Paola, Sophia, Amanda, and El Lobo, who gave their creative, youthful ALL with great joy and friendship to La Casa del Pan. Thanks especially to Amy for managing with creativity, skill, and love in Mexico City. Thanks to Rodrigo for all his help, poetry, and inspiration. Big thanks to my compadre, Octavio Barocio, for making me open La Casa del Pan in the first place, for designing the Ecological Park and Tlalpuente, and for all his great ideas and eternal optimism. Thanks to Cristian for all the hours he humorously put in for the cause. Warmest thanks to my neighbors and best friends, Maku and Javier de María y Campos, and to Javier's mother, Cuca. Thanks to my hermano Julio Delgado, who instructed me on recipes and restaurants. Thanks to Nelva for teaching me to make great pozole. Thanks to Beti for steering the ship through rough waters, making cookies with one hand, serving coffee with another, and selling bread with a third. Deepest thanks to my friend Isaac Bejar, owner of Saks Natural Restaurant in Mexico City, who first showed me how a fine restaurant is run in every aspect of the business. I am most grateful to him for his very generous and expert help.

Many, many thanks to George and Jane Collier for making La Casa del Pan in San Cristobal possible, for bringing us to Chiapas many years ago, for teaching us, and for believing in us. Special thanks to Fernando Ochoa for being the greatest landlord and friend I could have wished for. Thanks to Jose Luis for helping me get oriented in the restaurant business in San Cristobal and for being a good neighbor at all times. Thanks to Teresa Asnar for making the Ecological Park possible and for putting up some obstacles to overcome.

Thanks from my heart to Geshela, Jangchub, and Juan Carlos for spiritual guidance. Thanks to Flora and Janequi and Margarita for giving cooking classes and singing with me. Thanks to all my students over the years for all they taught me. Thanks to Philippe for making so much possible. Thanks to Cisco for his outstanding lettuce, herbs, seeds, suggestions, and photos, and to Mags for her happy company. Thanks to Warner for the beautiful portrait. Thanks to Nina Diakova for the precious gift of her painting of La Casa del Pan. Thanks to Melissa for cooking divinely and making everyone feel at home in the restaurant. Thanks to Gabi for making music with me and to both her and Igor for teaching me how to make papadzules.

Thanks to Max and Edna Nigh, who taught me about life as well as cooking, and who supported us as a family. Thanks to Steve and Nancy for their encouragement and for the cookbooks. Thanks to my dad, who taught me how to work and to operate a small business with generosity and vision. Thanks to my fellow mucisicans, Marguerite, Gabi, Alejandro, Hector, Manuel, Checo, Guido, Franco, Beto, Luis, Honorio, and Jorge for all the concerts in both Las Casas del Pan in Mexico City and San Cristobal. Thanks to Jorge for a great job of managing and to Sonia for helping out. Thanks to Maru for painting with me, and thanks also to Barbara. Thanks to Nuke for the greatest mural. Thanks to Asha, Amy, and Ian for being the best kids a mother could want and the inspiration for so much cooking.

Thanks to my wonderful editors, Bob and Cynthia Holzapfel, who are fun and brilliant and who made this book happen. Thanks to Michael Cook for going over it with a magnifying glass, over and over again. Finally, I wish to thank my dear friend Dorothy Bates for the idea, constant encouragement and guidance for this book. Her joyous experience in the kitchen is contagious, and I am indebted to her.

A Mayan Kitchen

Introduction

What makes Mexican cooking so delicious?—that is, authentic Mexican cooking, like the *sopes* you may remember eating in Oaxaca. The answer is love. It is the one essential ingredient to truly delicious food anywhere, and traditional Mexican cuisine abounds with it. For example, instead of throwing garlic, onion, and tomato in a blender before cooking them, try roasting them whole in a dry skillet before they go into the blender. See for yourself what a difference that little step makes in the taste. Try it to marimba music from Chiapas or to Jarocho harp from Veracruz.

This book, written for people living in the U.S., is not about American Mexican cooking, but is a guide to preparing delicious, highly nutritious, and authentic Mexican food, without the addition of meat.

Caring steps and exquisite seasonings are the loving details that put Mexican cooking in a class by itself. But what about the basic ingredients? Mexico has a richly diverse climate, with mineral-rich soils and heavy, seasonal rains. The soil bears robust harvests of a seemingly endless variety of delicious fruits and vegetables, which go fresh into the recipes. Traditionally, all crops were grown organically, but since the introduction of agribusiness and industrialized farming, there is now much chemically grown produce in the marketplace. Tomatoes and grapes in particular should always be carefully washed to remove as many residues as possible. I recommended seeking out organically-grown produce, whenever possible.

Mexican food is also some of the most nutritious in the world. It is based on the protein-rich bean-and-corn combination, with the addition of fresh vegetables and fruits. Oil is widely used, but it is not an indigenous ingredient, as it was introduced by the Spanish. Traditional Indian cooking uses little or no oil. In these recipes, I have reduced the oil to the minimum for health reasons, although for San Cristobal Bread Casserole, I couldn't get it below ½ cup, but a little indulgence must be allowed in that case!

One thing more: There is not *one* Mexico, but many. Each geographical region, with its unique climate and history, has developed its own cuisine. It would take more than one lifetime to experience all the recipes from all the regions. It would take more than one volume to enumerate the pleasures of each one.

This book is offered not only as a humble introduction to the wide world of Mexican cooking, but Mexican cooking without the use of meat. In recipes traditionally based on meat, adaptations to the recipes were made, in some cases substituting textured vegetable protein made from soybeans. The argument for a vegetarian diet is clear: it is healthful, being largely free of chemicals and hormones and low in fat as well. A diversified vegetarian diet using unrefined foods is high in fiber, which is essential to the maintenance of good health and a proven preventative of many kinds of cancer.

I became a vegetarian gradually, by inclination rather than by force. I prefer fruits, grains, and vegetables to meat. I've been making whole-grain bread at home in Mexico for twenty-five years. It has been one of my life's pleasures. I still eat meat on occasion (as a dinner guest, for example). I stopped buying it to prepare for my family when it no longer appealed to me. I looked for vegetarian recipes that would satisfy my adolescents' appetites and preferences. I started inventing recipes, adapted from traditional Mexican cooking, substituting the meat and reducing the fat. In 1989, I opened La Casa del Pan in Mexico City (in the Ecological Park of Loreto and Pena Pobre, on the corner of Insurgentes Sur and Ave. San Fernando, in Tlalpan), where I trained a staff of dedicated Mexican men and women to prepare healthful, whole-grain breads, vegetarian pastries, and chemical-free, low-sugar jams and vegetable conserves. In 1993, we moved to San Cristobal de las Casas, where I opened another Casa del Pan, this time with a restaurant as well as a bakery. Everything we serve is made fresh, using local and home-grown produce. We prefer to buy from organic growers. We believe that we are what we eat, and this principle guides us toward a wholesome diet.

I wish I could somehow include within these pages the melodious sound of the Chiapas marimba, the Jarocho harp of Veracruz, the Huapango guitar of the Huasteca, and the Mayan flute and drum of the central highlands of Chiapas. Music is an integral part of this book.

Kippy Nigh
San Cristobal de Las Casas

A Word About Ingredients

Most of the ingredients for the recipes in this book can be found in supermarkets and farmers' markets. Look in the specialty sections for dried chiles, and ask your merchants for the various types you need. Dried chiles keep well in cool, dry storage, so stock up to have them on hand. Mexican restaurants are good places to inquire where some of the more unusual ingredients are to be found. There are, however, some things which are only available in Mexico, and even there, only in certain areas. A few recipes using these ingredients have been included for their nutritional, culinary, or historical interest. In these special cases substitutions are suggested.

To help familiarize you with Mexican foods and where they may be found, the following glossary is offered.

Achiote (ah-chee-oh´-tay): This is a small, dark red seed which is ground and sold in a paste form in a small box. It is mild in flavor and intense in color. Look for it in Mexican markets and specialty shops.

Amaranth (Amaranto) (ah-mah-ran´-toh): A tiny, yellow grain, native to pre-Hispanic Mexico. It once occupied a place equal in importance to beans in the Mexican diet. Aztec cooks toasted it, ground it, and incorporated it into corn dough for making tortillas and tamales. This grain possesses the highest percentage of protein of any known grain. Its amino acids are in well-balanced proportions for human nutritional needs. Unfortunately, the grain was banned by colonizing Spaniards, on pain of death for its cultivation, because of its use in rituals honoring non-Christian gods. Toasted amaranth was mixed with honey and then molded into dolls, which were then offered to the gods on home altars. Luckily, this valuable grain survived its religious persecution and is now making a comeback. Amaranth is available in health food stores and organic seed catalogs.

Ate (ah´-tay): A paste made by boiling down guava or quince with raw sugar. It is served with *queso fresco* (fresh cheese) after dinner. Sold in Mexican markets at the cheese stands.

Bolillos (boh-lee´-yohz): Crusty white rolls used in Mexico to make tortas (sandwiches) of all kinds.

amaranth

Cajeta (cah-heh´-tah): Caramelized goat's milk, made by boiling down the milk with sugar over a period of several hours until it turns golden brown. It can be eaten alone (in small amounts) or as a topping for crepes or ice cream. It is sold in many supermarkets, as well as in Mexican markets and specialty stores

Camote (kah-moh´-tay): Sweet potatoes—in Mexico there are two main varieties—white and orange.

Chayote (chaiy-oh´-tay): A light green, pear-shaped vegetable that grows on a vine, up and over trees and trellises. Some varieties have spines, some do not. Used in soups and stews, or alone.

chayotes

Chihuahua cheese (chee-wah´-wah): A white cheese similar in flavor to white cheddar. It was originally introduced in the state of Chihuahua by the Mennonites. It melts nicely.

Chiles (chee´-lays): These are so numerous in variety and so important to Mexican cooking that they deserve their own section, beginning on page 16.

Chipilín (chee-pee-leen´): A mild, small-leafed herb used to make soups and tamales in southern Mexico since pre-Hispanic days. Its Latin name is *Crotalaria longitostrata*. Chipilín may be impossible to find outside of Mexico. It is used fresh. Watercress can be used as a substitute.

Cilantro (see-lan´-troh): Fresh coriander leaves, often labeled in supermarkets as Chinese parsley. It looks similar to normal parsley but is very pungent. Available in most stores.

Colorin (coh-loh-reen´): Scarlet, saber-shaped flowers that grow on a leguminous tree. They come out in the spring, before the leaves.

Cueza (kway´-sah): The thick, starchy root of the chayote vine.

Epazote (eh-pah-zoh´-tay): The Latin name for *epazote* is *Chenopodium ambrosiocles*. In English, this herb is known as "wormwood," and is a remedy for worms. Many Mexican recipes use it, but it's difficult to find in the U.S., except at Mexican farmers' markets. It is an easy-to-grow perennial.

epazote

Fideos (fee-day´-ohs): Fine, vermicelli-type pasta, used in soups.

Guanabana (wah-nah´-bah-nah): A grapefruit-sized, geodesically-shaped fruit that is dusky green on the outside and creamy white with large, shiny black seeds on the inside.

Guava (wah´-vah): This fruit, the size of limes or of lemons, is yellow in color, and has tiny yellow seeds. It is a very aromatic fruit and is very popular in Mexico, where it is used to make hot punch, ate, and popsicles, among other treats.

Guaunsoncles (wahn-sohn´-clays): Large, green, tiny-budded flower clusters which are stuffed with cheese, dipped in batter, and fried before being eaten by pulling the stem through the teeth. They are very difficult to find outside of Mexico.

Hierba santa (yier´-bah san´-tah): Latin name, *Piper sp.* "Hierba santa" means "holy herb," a name given to it for its medicinal properties as a cure for stomach ache, antidote for poison, and a stimulant for fevers. The root is the part used for medicine. In Chiapas, the herb is known by the Maya indians as *mumo* or *mumun*, where it is used as a wrapping to steam bean tamales. It is a large, wide, dark green leaf, about the size of one's hand with the fingers spread out. It is very pleasingly aromatic. It is not sold in the United States.

Huitlacoche (weet-lah-koh´-chay): This is a Mexican delicacy. In the U.S., corn farmers call this black fungus "corn smut" and throw it away, but in Mexico, farmers actually promote its growth. Canned, it is available in many supermarkets in the canned foods or Mexican specialty sections. Also available fresh in Mexican farmers' markets in the southwest U.S. during summer and fall.

Jamaica (hah-may´-kah): Sold dried, this is the dark red hibiscus flower. It is used to make iced tea and is similar to cranberries in taste. It is very high in vitamin C.

Jícama (hee´-kah-mah): This is a root vegetable, white in color, with a thin, light brown skin. It comes in all sizes, from the size of a lime to the size of a cantaloupe. It is beet-shaped. It is usually eaten raw in Mexico, but it makes a good substitute for water chestnuts in Chinese cooking. Available in many supermarkets.

Lima (lee´-mah): A delicately flavored, pale green to light yellow citrus fruit. They fruits vary in size from a large lemon to a small orange. They are used to make Sopes de Lima in the Yucatan.

Maguey (mah-gay´): Called a century plant in English, this variety of cactus has long, fleshy green spears that radiate out, lotus fashion, from its heart and terminate in long, sharp needles. The Aztec priests used them to pierce their tongues and skin in initiation rites. The nectar that collects inside of the heart of the maguey is drunk fresh as *aguamiel* (ah´-gwah-myehl) or "honey water." When the honey water is boiled down for about 15 hours, it turns into a delicious syrup which has medicinal properties for the throat, bronchial tubes, and stomach and is an ideal sugar substitute for people with diabetes. When the honey water is allowed to ferment for three days, it becomes *pulque*, a mildly alcoholic drink.

Mamey (mah-may´): This fruit looks like a small, rough-skinned, dusty brown football on the outside. Inside, when it is at its peak of ripeness, it is an intense, fiery orange color. It is very difficult to pick out the good ones, which is why, in the markets in Mexico, the vendors cut them open so their clients can see what they're getting. It has a creamy, rich texture and exotic flavor.

Manchego cheese (mahn-chay´-go): Originally from Spain, this smooth, mild, white cheese melts well. Muenster cheese can be used as a substitute.

Mango (mahng´-goh): There are many varieties of this fruit available in Mexico. The kind most commonly exported is called *manila*, and it is readily available now in most stores in the U.S. during the spring and summer months.

Manzanilla (mahn-sahn-ee´-yah): The dried flowers of chamomile make a pleasant tea that aids digestion and cures acid stomach and some kinds of cramps.

Masa (mah´-sah): Corn dough used for making tortillas. It is traditionally prepared by boiling dried corn with lime, which makes the protein in the corn more available for human nutrition. The corn is then washed under running water and ground into a paste, adding water as necessary to achieve the right consistency. The supermarkets sell *instant masa*, which only requires the addition of water to produce masa.

Masa hojaldre (mah´-sah oh-hahl´-dray): Flaky pastry dough.

Nopales (noh-pah´-lays): The fleshy, new pads of the prickly pear cactus (in Latin, *O. megacantha*) native to Mexico. They are very nutritious and their daily consumption helps to control diabetes. They're delicious in soups, salads, eggs, and main dishes. They grow in warm, dry climates. These are sometimes available fresh in supermarkets. Pick tender, young pads. Handle them with tongs and remove the spines with a sharp knife employed at an angle. They are widely available in canned form in the specialty sections of most supermarkets. They are also called *nopalitos* when they are very tender.

Piloncillo (Pee-lohn-see´-yoh): Dark brown, unrefined cane sugar sold in hard, cone-shaped blocks. To use it, either melt it with a small amount of water or grate it. It is good in punch. Piloncillo is available only in Mexican markets and some health food stores.

Pepitas (peh-pee´-tahs): Squash seeds, sold raw by the pound in supermarkets and health food stores. Also sold roasted and salted for appetizers.

Pipian (pee-pee´-ahn): A powder made from grinding pepitas and salt together. Sometimes dried chiles are added to the grinding. This is used to make pipian sauce for using in papadzules and other recipes. Sold in the specialty section of supermarkets and in Mexican markets. It is also sold bottled.

Pithaya (pee-tay´-yah): A hot-pink fruit, about the size of a grapefruit, with a thin skin divided into sections. Inside, it has small, black seeds throughout. Juicy and mild.

Platano macho (plah´-tah-noh mah´-choh): Plantain—used for cooking, it can usually be found in large supermarkets. It has a bitter taste when raw, but cooked it's delicious.

Pozole (poh-zoh´-lay): Hominy corn is used for making a hearty soup by the same name. You can buy it both dried and cooked.

Pulque (pool´-kay): An alcoholic beverage produced by fermenting the nectar that collects in the heart of the maguey. It is not distilled. It is possibly the oldest alcoholic beverage produced in North America, where it was once widely used. Many Mexican recipes employ *pulque*, but it is not exported, since it does not keep well. Beer makes an acceptable substitute.

Romeritos (roh-mehr-ee´-tohs): A feathery, leafy green used to make a traditional Christmas stew. Only available in Mexico.

Rompope (rohm-poh´-pay): A Mexican eggnog, sold bottled in specialty shops.

Sangrita (san-gree´-tah): A tomato-chile drink traditionally served with tequila. The product sold bottled in liquor stores does not compare with the homemade product.

Tomatillo (toh-mah-tee´-yoh): A small, green variety of tomato, which grows encased with a thin husk. It is commonly used for making green salsa. Tomatillos are not underripe tomatoes.

Tuna (too´-nah): The fruit of the prickly pear cactus. Found in some large supermarkets and farmers' markets when in season (early spring).

Vanilla (Vainilla) (baiy-nee´-yah): The bean produced by an orchid native to Mexico. It grows in the tropical rain forest. The process of drying the beans for market is long and labor-intensive, which makes real vanilla very expensive.

Zapote (sah-poh´-tay): There are many varieties of this tropical fruit, some black, some brown, some orange, and some yellow. These and innumerable other tropical fruits are sold in Mexico's markets, but seldom reach the rest of the world, due to their fragility.

Chiles

Chiles are native to Mexico, where more than 100 varieties are estimated to grow throughout the country's mountains and valleys. Of these, less than 10 are sold commercially in the United States. In Mexico, many more varieties can be obtained, especially in Mexico City's markets where produce from the entire country is sold.

Chiles have been an important part of the Mexican diet for hundreds of years, as archaeologists have discovered. When the Spanish colonists visited Mexican markets, they were astounded at the quantity and variety of chiles (as well as other produce) traded and consumed by the indigenous population. They recorded the following legend about a chile merchant:

In Tula, where Huëmac, (the last of the Toltec kings) reined, a certain chile seller from an outlying region arrived to offer his chiles for sale. As was the custom in his region of Huasteca, he wore no clothes at all. When the daughter of King Huëmac saw him, she fell ill with desire. Her whole body became swollen, and she had to be taken home and put to bed immediately. When the king learned that his daughter was sick with love and by whom, he sent for the chile seller, whom he scolded severely for not wearing a *maxtlatl* to cover his nakedness. The chile seller answered him that nakedness was the custom of his region. The king then ordered him, "You have made my daughter sick with love; now you are responsible for curing her." So the chile seller had no choice but to cure the beautiful daughter of the king, and thus became his son-in-law. The numerous Toltec suitors of the princess, however, were very unhappy about the marriage and complained bitterly to the king, convincing him that the chile seller had had an unfair advantage over them, and besides, he was of a low class, much beneath the princess. The king grew ashamed of his new son-in-law and sent him off to war as a way of eliminating him. In battle, the Toltecs abandoned him in the midst of the enemy and returned to the king to tell him his son-in-law was dead. The chile seller, however, was victorious in battle, single-handedly killing many enemies, which made him the hero of the day, and the suitors had to eat their words. The king prepared a great feast to honor him, and the Toltecs, impressed as they were by his strength and bravery, accepted him as their countryman. The princess was credited with being the first to perceive that he was no ordinary chile seller, but the God Tezcatlipoca, who had once again fooled the Toltecs, as on other occasions. (From the book, *Capsicum y Cultura: La Historia del Chili*, by Janet Long-Solís, Fondo de Cultura Económica, Mexico)

The variety of chiles in Mexico is due to their regionalization over many years in the countless micro-climates that are created by changes in elevation, latitude, and rainfall throughout the country. But known to all Mexicans is the following list of the most readily found chiles, which are divided into two main categories, according to how they are used, fresh or dried.

Fresh Chiles

Chilaca (chee-la´-ka): This chile is dark brown or chocolate, has an undulated surface, and is narrow, long, and often curving. It has a mild flavor. It is used to make *rajas* (strips of chile) for soups or to put in tacos or quesadillas. Often, these *rajas* are prepared with cream and cheese. Ripened and dried, this chile becomes the chile "pasilla."

Guëro (wey´-do): This chile is popular in Tabasco, Veracruz, and the Yucatan Peninsula where it is used in sauces which employ tomatoes, green olives, and capers. It is pale yellow, ranges from 2 to 5 inches in length, and is about ¾ inch wide. It is mildly hot and has an excellent flavor.

Habanero (ah-bahn-ey´-do): This chile from the Yucatan Peninsula and the Caribbean is the hottest of all, but is the only one that is not irritating to the lining of a sensitive stomach. It is of the genus *Capsicum sinense* (all of the other chiles listed are of the genus *Capsicum annum*). It must be eaten in very small amounts, since it is fire itself. It has a triangular shape and is about ½ to 2 inches long. It has a smooth, undulated surface, comes in shades of green, orange, and red, and is very beautiful to see. It lends a wonderful aroma to hot sauces. Dilute it well with lime juice and salt.

Jalapeño (ha-la-peya´-yo): This is a medium green chile, smooth and gently tapered to a rounded tip. On the average, it is about 2½ inches long and about ¾ inch wide. It is medium-hot. The *jalapeño* gets its name from the city of Jalapa, the capital of the state of Veracruz, where it has been popular since colonial times. It is used fresh or occasionally scorched first on a dry skillet or comal (a round plate of unglazed pottery or tin, upon which tortillas are traditionally cooked).

Manzano (mahn-sahn´-no): This is a wide chile shaped like an apple (*manzano* means apple in Spanish). It is normally about 3 inches wide and 3 inches long, light green to yellow and sometimes orange and red in color. It can be very hot. It is usually eaten fresh, although it makes a nice addition to cooked sauces.

Poblano (po-blah´-no): This is a large, dark green chile used for stuffing. It is conical in shape, undulated, and varies in size from 3-5 inches long. It varies from mild to hot. You can tell you have a hot one if it burns your fingers as you are deveining it. To prepare, first scorch it on a *comal*, in an oven, or over an open flame. Then put it into a bag to sweat for a few minutes, peel, seed, and devein. Ripened and dried, it becomes the *chile ancho*.

Serrano (say-rrah´-no): This chile is smaller than the jalapeño, smooth, medium green to orange, and about 1½ inches long by ½ inch wide. Serrano chiles are hotter than jalapeños, with a stronger flavor. It is used fresh or scorched, and is very popular in *salsas* with any meal.

Dried Chiles

Ancho (an´cho): This chile is used widely for making *mole*, the dark sauce originally from Puebla and now made in many parts of Mexico. *Mole* has many variations. It averages 4 inches in length, and is about 3 inches wide at the top, tapering to a point. Very wrinkled and dark reddish-brown in color, it has a slightly acid, pungent flavor, and ranges from mild to spicy hot. It is first softened in enough hot water to cover, then sliced open to remove the seeds. It is most commonly ground to make sauce and makes a great meal when stuffed.

Cascabel (kas-kah´-behl): Cascabel means rattle, which is what the chile does when shaken. It is round, about 1 inch in diameter, dark brown, and has a smooth, thin skin. It is mildly spicy and lends a unique flavor to sauces when roasted and ground.

Catarina (cah-tah-ree´-nah): This chile is similar to cascabel in color, size, and flavor, but it is triangular in shape.

Chipotle (chee-poht´-lay): Jalapeños, when dried and smoked, become chipotles. It is about 2 inches long, ¾ inch wide, and is a dusty brown when dried. Pickled, they make a wonderful hot relish The most delicious ones are pickled at home. The commercial chipotles are made from *chile moro*, a dried, dark red chile. Sold in cans throughout Mexico and the U.S., chipotles make a tasty addition to soups, sauces, and salad dressings. Use them sparingly; they may be hot.

De Arbol (day ahr´-bohl): This beautiful red chile, 2½ inches long and ½ inch wide, when roasted and ground, lends delicious heat to many sauces that are served throughout Mexico. It is easily found in the Mexican sections of U.S. markets.

Guajillo (wah-hee´-yo): There are two types of *chile guajillo*: hot and mild. If it is not specified, assume they are hot until you have tried them. Both types are long, smooth, dark reddish brown, and thin skinned. The seeds rattle when the dried chiles are shaken. They are about 4 inches long and 1½ inches wide. They give a great flavor to soups and sauces; soften first in hot water and then grind and strain.

Moro (mo´-roh): A dark red, pungent chile that is usually about 1 x 1½ inches.

Mulato (moo-la´-toh): Similar in size and shape to the ancho, it has a brownish-black color. It may be used in place of the *ancho chile* to create a slightly sweeter and darker mole sauce.

Pasilla (pah-see´-yah): When the *chilaca* is dried, it becomes the chile pasilla. It is dark brown to nearly black and is wonderful for adding flavorful heat to sauces and soups. It is long, narrow, and very wrinkled. It is sometimes called *chile negro*.

Pequín (pee-keen´): This tiny ¼-inch chile packs heat. Bright red in color, round and smooth, they are beautiful to look at. Ground to make a powder, they make great *salsa picante* to accompany *tostadas*, *tamales*, and *sopes*. They are used in many recipes in this book.

About Tortillas

The most important element in the Mexican diet is the corn tortilla. Without tortillas, a meal is not complete. Every peasant girl learns how to pat out good tortillas by the time she is ten years old, but the girls are practicing long before that.

When we lived in a Mayan Indian village in the 1970s, I had plenty of time to practice patting out tortillas while the girls and women laughed at my efforts, patiently teaching me over and over again. Working with those women, I learned how to enjoy the moment. I also learned how to make tortillas and liked it so much that when my family moved to the city, I continued to make them every day on the stove's griddle.

When we made tortillas in the village, someone would first build up the fire. (For tortilla-making, high heat is required.) The fire, which was on a dirt floor in the middle of a one-room wattle and daub house, never went out. Sometimes it was left to dwindle down, but the red-hot coals underneath the ashes could always be uncovered and blown upon to ignite more firewood.

The corn was prepared the day before by boiling it with lime powder. A dough was made by grinding the cooked corn using a rotary, cast iron grinder. (My mother-in-law purchased one for our hosts and carried it out to the village herself, an eight-hour trek).

To obtain the fine consistency required for superior tortillas, the dough was then ground again on a *metate*, a stone slab, with a *mano*, a stone roller. I raised big blisters on my hands when I first ground corn this way. The metate can be used for the first grinding as well, but it is arduous and time-consuming work.

Once the corn was ground finely enough, water was worked into the dough using a kneading motion until a soft, smooth consistency was obtained. To assure that the right amount of water had been added, a ball was formed with about a quarter of a cup of dough. This was then patted out to determine its pliancy. If the dough is too dry, the tortilla cracks at the edges; if the dough is too wet, it sticks to the fingers and palms. It's better to add the water gradually, to obtain the right consistency. Otherwise, you can easily add too much water, and end up with a sticky, hard-to-handle dough.

When the dough was ready and the fire was blazing fiercely, the *comal* (an unglazed earthenware or tin plate, averaging 3 feet in diameter) was placed over the fire, supported by three large stones placed at equal distance from each other around the fire. The comal was first painted with a thick lime-water solution so that the tortillas would not stick and would inflate more easily during cooking. Then began the ritual of tortilla-patting and baking.

If the family is large, this becomes a party, as girls of all ages pat and place their tortillas on the comal, taking turns turning the tortillas over as they bake. Tortillas are always made at home in the villages.

For hundreds of years the grinding of corn has been the first human sound in the morning in the Mayan villages of Chiapas. The pre-dawn silence is broken with its rhythmic, meditative quality, accented occasionally by the roosters' crowing. To one accustomed to it, it is just a part of life, like all the other subsistence chores. The women of our household did their work cheerfully and leisurely, sharing the load. Their attitude toward work, which many would consider drudgery, was admirable.

In recent years, life in rural Mexico has been changing. Mills now grind the corn in many communities. Roads make the transportation of instant corn dough possible. Technology has brought many conveniences, but there has also been a considerable decline in quality of the masa (due to the way the corn is now processed).

Nowadays, dehydrated, instant tortilla flour is sold by the 100-pound sackful throughout Mexico. Many peasant women consider this "modern" and prefer it to boiling and grinding their own corn, unaware of the health menace which this inferior product presents.

If corn is not boiled with lime when it is processed, many of the nutrients in the corn cannot be metabolized by the human body. If tortillas are the mainstay of the diet, as they still are for the majority of Mexicans, using instant tortilla dough may create a niacin deficiency, which leads to pellagra, a debilitating condition that can be fatal if left untreated.

The combination of beans and lime-treated corn creates a well-balanced proportion of the amino acids needed to meet human protein requirements. Traditional varieties of corn and beans make a meal that is high in fiber and carbohydrates and provides high-energy fuel that is healthful for the digestive tract. People who live on a diet of high-quality tortillas and beans have a strong build and sound teeth. One study from Honduras showed that the very best diet for preventing the onset of "modern" diseases—heart disease, hypertension, diabetes, etc.—is a diet based on corn and beans. Unfortunately, industrialized food, grains grown with agricultural chemicals, and highly-sugared bottled beverages are being sold throughout Mexico, and the adverse health effects of these products are now becoming apparent.

To make your own tortillas from scratch, purchase dried corn (hominy or field corn, not popcorn). The following recipe provides the amount of lime required in proportion to the corn used. The number of tortillas produced depends upon how large you make them and how thick. Beginner's tortillas are usually thicker than those made by veterans.

How to Make Tortillas from Scratch

This recipe will yield about 40 five-inch tortillas, depending on how thick you make them. With practice, you can produce delicately thin tortillas that puff during baking on the comal or griddle. Don't be discouraged if they don't puff up. Even the pros have occasional tortillas that don't puff. *Any* tortilla that you produce following this recipe will taste good, far superior to the factory-produced tortillas which tend to be hard and dry. If you can, make them with someone else, a child or a friend; it's so much more fun. (Ideally, learn the practice directly from someone who is skilled at making them.)

2.2 pounds (1 kilogram) dried corn
1 rounded tablespoon lime
1 cup water to dissolve the lime
water to cover the corn
large, unglazed earthenware pot, or an enamel or stainless steel pot (don't use aluminum)
rotary cast-iron corn grinder
tortilla press
clear plastic bag, cut into two circles the diameter of the tortilla press

Pick through the corn carefully to remove small stones or debris. Dissolve the lime in the cup of water, being careful to avoid contact with your eyes. Place the corn in the pot, and cover with water to about 2 inches above the corn. Place over high heat and boil for about 2 hours, or until the corn is barely tender and the skin pulls off easily. Remove from the heat and allow the corn to soak overnight in its cooking water. The next day, rinse and drain the corn two or three times. Now it is ready for grinding.

To grind the corn at home, you will need a rotary grinder that screws onto the edge of a work table. If you can, obtain a *metate* and find someone to teach you how to use it. Grind the corn first in the rotary mill, and then give it the final grinding on the metate to obtain the smoothest dough. Otherwise, two or even three grindings through the rotary grinder will be necessary. If you live near a tortilla factory, perhaps you can have the people there grind your corn for you. This will save you time and effort.

Once ground, the corn becomes *masa*. Add water in small amounts, then knead the dough until it is soft and silky smooth, but not sticky. To test the consistency, roll about ¼ cup of the dough into a ball, and flatten it out. It should be easy to manage.

If you choose to use *masa harina*, to make about 20 tortillas mix:

2 cups masa harina
1⅓ cups water

When your dough is ready, prepare your comal or griddle. A large rectangular pancake griddle is ideal for making tortillas on the stove. If it is well-seasoned (or non-stick), it will not need the thick lime-water solution that is used on traditional comals (page 19). Heat it to its hottest.

Meanwhile, roll approximately ¼ cup of dough into a ball. Place this in the center of one of the pieces of plastic, on the press. Now place the other piece of plastic on top. Close the press and push the handle down firmly over the top. Open the press and check to see if the tortilla is uniformly thin. If not, rotate it and press again. With practice, you'll get it just right. Open the press and peel off the top piece of plastic. Then lift the tortilla together with the bottom piece of plastic, and lay it on your outspread hand, plastic on top. Now peel off the plastic, and lay the tortilla on the griddle or comal, as shown. Veterans transfer the wet tortilla from one hand to the other, positioning it for ideal placement on the comal. Refinements in your technique will come with practice.

In the beginning, I suggest making tortillas like the Guatemalans do—thick. They are easier to handle, and you'll be more likely to repeat the process.

Once the tortilla is on the griddle, a second ball of dough may be formed. Then, turn the tortilla on the griddle as soon as it is possible to lift an edge without breaking it. Press your second ball of dough, and check the tortilla on the griddle. The second side should bake the longest, cooking the tortilla through. Place the second tortilla beside the first. The first tortilla may now be ready for its second and final turn. If all conditions and requirements are met, it should puff up. As soon as it does, remove it and place it inside a cotton napkin to keep warm while you make the rest of the tortillas.

Ideally, someone with experience should help you to learn, but don't get discouraged if it seems difficult at first. Just keep trying, like when you first learned to ride a bicycle!

A Mayan woman makes tortillas over a wood fire on the floor of her house.

Appetizers

Antojitos

Chalupas

Serves 6-8
Preparation time: 15 minutes

18 small corn tortillas (about 3
  inches in diameter)
½ cup sunflower or safflower
  oil for frying
1 cup refried beans
2 carrots, boiled and chopped
2 beets, boiled and chopped
½ onion, thinly sliced
6 radishes, chopped
3 tablespoons cilantro or parsley,
  chopped
1 cup shredded lettuce
Mild or Hot Ranchero Sauce
  (pages 146, 147) or Fresh
  Mexican Chile Sauce (page 142)
  or Green Chile Sauce (page 144)
sea salt to taste

These chalupas, from San Cristobal de las Casas, Chiapas, can serve as a light supper accompanied with beans and rice, or as an appetizer to a larger meal. They are great for parties, because they go a long way.

Fry both sides of the tortilla in the heated oil until crispy. Drain on paper towels and arrange on a tray. Spread each tortilla with refried beans, and cover with carrots, beets, onion, radishes, cilantro, lettuce, sauce, and salt to taste.

Per serving: Calories: 170, Protein: 5 gm., Fat: 4 gm., Carbohydrates: 27 gm.

Roasted Peanuts with Garlic and Chile

Cacahuates con Ajo y Chile

This appetizer is served in some of Mexico's best hotel bars as a botana (free snack) to accompany the drinks.

Combine the peanuts, chiles, and garlic, and sauté in the oil until the garlic is cooked. Add the salt. This can be made days ahead of time and kept in a paper bag.

Per serving: Calories: 346, Protein: 11 gm., Fat: 28 gm., Carbohydrates: 9 gm.

Serves 6-8
Preparation time: 10 minutes

1 pound Spanish peanuts (with the skins still on)
10 whole dried de arbol chiles
10 cloves garlic, minced
2 tablespoons sunflower oil
fine-grain sea salt

Nachos

Here's a nutritious, delicious recipe that kids can make for their friends, provided you keep the ingredients on hand.

Arrange the tostada chips on an oven proof platter, and sprinkle the cheese on top.
Bake at 400°F for 5 minutes. Serve with the salsa.

Per serving: Calories: 112, Protein: 5 gm., Fat: 6 gm., Carbohydrates: 8 gm.

Variation: Spoon hot black beans over the nachos just before serving.

Serves 4
Preparation time: 10 minutes

2 cups tostada chips
½ cup grated cheddar or jack or Chihuahua cheese
Guadalajara Hot Sauce (page 143) or Fresh Mexicana Chile Sauce (page 142) to taste

Jicama with Lime and Chile

Jicama con Limón y Chile

Serves 6-8
Preparation time: 10 minutes

1 pound jícama, peeled and cut
  into ¼-inch slices
juice of 5 green limes, or 2
  lemons
½ teaspoon powdered chile
  pequín
fine grain sea salt to taste

Jícama is a juicy, white, starchy root with a thin, light beige skin. It is crispy and takes on flavors very easily. This is a refreshing appetizer on a hot afternoon.

Arrange the jícama slices on a platter. Sprinkle the lime juice on top, followed by the chile and salt. Simple and non-fat!

Per serving: Calories: 33, Protein: 0 gm., Fat: 0 gm., Carbohydrates: 8 gm.

Green Mangos with Lime and Chile

Mango Verde con Limón y Chile

Serves 6
Preparation time: 10 minutes

1 pound green mangos, peeled
  and cut into thick strips
juice of 3 limes
½ teaspoon powdered chile
  pequín
fine grain sea salt to taste

Select underripe, firm mangos for this tart appetizer with exquisite flavor.

Arrange the mango strips on a platter. Sprinkle with lime juice, powdered chile, salt, and serve.

Per serving: Calories: 52, Protein: 0 gm., Fat: 0 gm., Carbohydrates: 12 gm.

Ron's Best Guacamole

Guacamole

The beauty of this guacamole is its simplicity. Use only the very ripest, but not overripe, avocados.

Mix the avocado with the chiles, add the lime juice and salt, mix well, and serve with tortilla chips.

Per serving: Calories: 207, Protein: 3 gm., Fat: 14 gm., Carbohydrates: 17 gm.

Serves 6-8
Preparation time: 10 minutes

4 ripe avocados, smashed with a fork
4 fresh jalapeño chiles, seeded and finely chopped
juice of 2 limes
½ teaspoon salt

Ron's Bean Dip

Botana de Frijól

If you are looking for an economical appetizer to please everyone, this is great. There are never any leftovers when this dip is served.

Sauté the onion and chile in the oil until the onion is transparent. Add the refried beans, heat through, and add bean broth or water to obtain the consistency desired. Finally, add the cheese and stir over low heat until it melts. Serve hot with tostada chips.

Per serving (dip only): Calories: 240, Protein: 7 gm., Fat: 15 gm., Carbohydrates: 16 gm.

Serves 6
Preparation time: 15 minutes

½ onion, sliced
⅓ cup fresh jalapeño chiles, minced
¼ cup safflower or sunflower oil
2 cups Refried Beans (page 123)
½ cup cheddar or Jack cheese, grated
tostada chips

Quesadillas

Serves 6
Preparation time: 20 minutes

Queso means cheese in Spanish, but these tasty appetizers are not necessarily made with cheese. They are popular throughout Mexico, and there are many variations. There are two basic ways of making them: with fresh tortilla dough or with already made tortillas. To make them with fresh tortilla dough, you will need a tortilla press. Quesadilla fillings are the same as those used for Empanadas (page 164) in the Breads section.

1 pound prepared masa harina dough for making tortillas, or
12 corn tortillas
filling:
  Mushroom Filling (page 165), Huitlacoche Filling (page 166), Squash Blossom Filling (page 167), Potato Filling (page 168), or grated Oaxaca, Swiss, or Chihuahua Cheese, or other filling
Mild or Hot Ranchero Sauce (pages 146, 147), Fresh Mexican Chile Sauce (page 142), or Green Chile Sauce (page 144)

Per quesadilla (with Mushroom Filling): Calories: 54, Protein: 1 gm., Fat: 2 gm., Carbohydrates: 7 gm.

Heat a comal (large tin plate for making tortillas) or a griddle over high heat.

Take ¼ cup of dough, and roll it into a ball. Place it on a small piece of a plastic bag on a tortilla press. Cover with another piece of plastic, and close the press firmly. Peel the top piece of plastic off the tortilla, then place the tortilla on your other hand, and peel off the other piece. Lay the tortilla on the griddle. Allow to cook for 5-10 seconds. Carefully lift one corner with your hand or a spatula to turn the tortilla over.

Place a spoonful of filling on one half of the tortilla, fold over the other half, and gently pinch the edges together. Cook the quesadilla on the edge of the griddle (where it is coolest) for 1 minute, then turn it over and cook for another minute. Repeat until all the dough has been made into quesadillas. Serve with the salsa(s) of your choice.

To make quesadillas with ready-made tortillas, heat a comal or griddle over high heat. Place a tortilla on the comal for 10 seconds, turn it over, and put a spoonful of filling on ½ of the tortilla. Fold over the other half, and cook for 1 minute; then turn over and cook for another minute. Serve with the salsa(s) of your choice.

Barbara's Catalanian Eggplant

Berenjena Catalána de Barbara

Berenjena is Spanish for eggplant. This recipe was taught to me by my friend, Barbara Torres, from Barcelona, Spain. Her family speaks Catalán, the dialect of Barcelona, at their home in Mexico City.

Serves 4
Preparation time: 20 minutes

Roast the eggplant in a dry skillet over medium heat, turning to brown evenly. It should be well browned. Peel and cut into strips lengthwise. Arrange on a plate, interspersed with the pimento strips. Sprinkle with the olive oil, salt, and black pepper. Serve with hot whole grain bread or crusty bolillos.

1 medium eggplant
1 red pimento, sliced in strips
¼ cup olive oil
sea salt to taste
freshly ground black pepper to taste

Per serving: Calories: 160, Protein: 1 gm., Fat: 13 gm., Carbohydrates: 9 gm.

Chile Yogurt Dip for Raw Vegetables

Salsa de Yogurt con Chile para Verduras Crudas

Makes 2¼ cups
Preparation time: 5 minutes

2 cups low-fat, plain yogurt
3 tablespoons olive oil (optional)
1 Tablespoon parsley, chopped
2 green onions with greens, chopped
dash of Worcestershire sauce
1 chipotle chile, chopped
¼ teaspoon freshly ground black pepper
sea salt to taste

Here's a low-fat, refreshing appetizer with a spicy kick.

Blend all the ingredients, and chill. Serve with chilled fresh vegetables: carrot strips, cucumber slices, cauliflower flowerets, broccoli flowerets, pimentos, jícama, etc.

Per 2 tablespoons: Calories: 21, Protein: 2 gm., Fat: 0 gm., Carbohydrates: 2 gm.

Jalapeño Jelly

Jalea de Jalapeño

Yield: 2 pints
Preparation time: 30 minutes

15 fresh green jalapeño chiles, seeded and minced (use a food processor)
1½ cups apple cider vinegar
5 cups unrefined sugar
1 bottle liquid pectin
cream cheese
crackers

Prepare the jelly ahead of time, and can in sterile jars. It makes a delicious and unusual gift.

In a large saucepan, heat the chiles, vinegar, and sugar to a boil, stirring constantly. Reduce the heat and simmer for 15 minutes. Remove from the heat and add the pectin. Return to the heat and simmer 3 more minutes. Turn off the heat and pour the hot jelly into hot, sterilized jars. Seal immediately. Place in a hot water bath which completely covers the jars, and boil for 15 minutes. Remove the jars after they have cooled.

Serve with cream cheese and crackers.

Per 2 tablespoons: Calories: 235, Protein: 0 gm.,
Fat: 0 gm., Carbohydrates: 57 gm.

jalapeños

Soups

Sopas

Tlalpeño Soup

Caldo Tlalpeno

Serves 5
Preparation time: 20 minutes
Cooking time: 2-3 hours

1 quart water
¼ pound garbanzos, soaked
  overnight
½ head of garlic, unpeeled
1 tablespoon sesame oil
2 cloves garlic, peeled and
  chopped
1 small onion, chopped
1 cup carrots, chopped
¼ pound fresh shiitake
  mushrooms, shredded
2 canned chipotle chiles,
  deseeded and cut in strips
1 sprig fresh epazote
1 teaspoon sea salt, or to taste
garnish:
1 avocado, peeled and cubed
1 tablespoon fresh cilantro,
  chopped
3 limes, cut in wedges
2 serrano chiles, deseeded and
  finely chopped

The unexpected combination of avocados and mushrooms in a fragrant broth with cilantro, epazote, and smoked chipotle chile, makes this garbanzo-based soup memorable.

Using a 2-quart pot, boil the garbanzos with the ½ head of garlic in 1 quart water until the garbanzos are tender. Heat the oil in a skillet, and sauté the 2 cloves of garlic, onion, and carrots for 5 minutes. Add these to the garbanzos, together with the mushrooms, chipotles, epazote, and salt. Cook for 20 minutes over medium heat. Serve in individual bowls over the avocado cubes, with the cilantro, limes, and serrano chiles on the side.

Per serving: Calories: 171, Protein: 4 gm., Fat: 7 gm., Carbohydrates: 20 gm.

epazote

San Cristobal Vegetable Soup

Sopa de Verdura

This recipe was first written down upon our return to San Cristobal in April of '93, (although it was born there many years before), inspired out of sheer joy and the desire to share.

Put the water on to boil. Sauté the onion and then the garlic and celery in the oil for 5 minutes over medium flame. Loosen the skins of the tomatoes by putting them in the boiling water for a few minutes, and then cold water. Peel, seed, and chop the tomatoes, and add to the onion and garlic, stirring occasionally. Add the Swiss chard and continue to stir for 5 minutes. Add the remaining ingredients and simmer for ½ hour.

Remove the chiles. If you want the soup to be spicy, blend the chiles with some of the broth and return to the soup. You can blend some of the vegetables to thicken the soup. Serve with hot, soft, warm tortillas wrapped in a cotton napkin, with Guadalajara Hot Sauce (page 143) on the side, a tossed green salad, and Chile-Black Bean Tamales (page 107) to complete the meal.

Per serving: Calories: 85, Protein: 1 gm., Fat: 4 gm., Carbohydrates: 11 gm.

Serves 6-8
Preparation time: 15 minutes
Cooking time: 40 minutes

3 quarts water
1 red onion, sliced
5 cloves garlic, chopped
1 cup celery, chopped
2 tablespoons olive oil
5 Italian tomatoes, peeled, seeded, and chopped
1 large bunch Swiss chard (¼ pound), chopped
3 carrots, chopped
1 chayote, chopped
½ cup fresh parsley, chopped
1 teaspoon fresh thyme, or ½ teaspoon dried
1 teaspoon oregano
2 small whole chipotle chiles
sea salt to taste

Vegetable Stock

Cosumé de Verdura

Makes 2 quarts
Preparation time: 15 minutes
Cooking time: 1 hour

1 onion, coarsely chopped
5 cloves garlic
3 tablespoons olive oil
3 ribs celery, chopped
2 medium tomatoes, coarsely chopped
3 quarts boiling water
3 zucchinis, sliced
3 carrots, sliced
½ pound green beans, chopped
2 potatoes, chopped
the celery tops
the carrot greens
leftover vegetables
1 teaspoon thyme
1 teaspoon oregano
1½ teaspoons sea salt

Prepare this the day you shop, either with newly bought vegetables, with the week's leftover odds and ends you want to use up, or both. Store in quart containers in the refrigerator (keeps well for four days) or in the freezer. Vegetable stock is a very tasty and handy addition to soups and sauces, instead of water.

Sauté the onion and garlic in the olive oil. Add the celery and tomatoes, and sauté until the tomatoes dissolve. Add the boiling water and the rest of the vegetables and seasonings. Simmer for 1 hour on low heat, and strain.

Per cup: Calories: 115, Protein: 2 gm., Fat: 5 gm., Carbohydrates: 16 gm.

Tortilla Soup

Sopa de Tortilla

This is a delicious way to use leftover tortillas. It is the most frequently ordered soup at La Casa del Pan.

Serves 4
Preparation time: 20 minutes
Cooking time: 25 minutes

Sauté the garlic and onion in 2 tablespoons oil. Add the tomatoes and chile, and sauté until the tomatoes dissolve. Blend and strain through a medium mesh strainer. Add 5 cups water and the epazote, and simmer for 25 minutes.

While the broth is cooking, heat ¼ cup oil in a skillet, and fry the tortilla strips until crisp, turning to brown both sides. Drain on paper towels. Place the tortilla strips in bowls with the cheese and avocado on top. Ladle the hot broth into the bowls, and serve with the chopped green onions and Guadalajara Hot Sauce on the side.

Per serving: Calories: 306, Protein: 5 gm., Fat: 18 gm., Carbohydrates: 31 gm.

3 cloves garlic, peeled and minced
1 medium onion, sliced
2 tablespoons corn, sunflower, or sesame oil
½ pound tomatoes, peeled, seeded, and chopped
1 huajillo chile
5 cups water
1 sprig fresh epazote
¼ cup corn or sesame oil
6 corn tortillas, cut in strips
¼ pound Jack cheese, chopped in squares (optional)
1 large ripe avocado, cut in slices
3 green onions, chopped
Guadalajara Hot Sauce (page 143)

Tortilla Soup with Chile Pasillo

Sopa de Tortilla con Chile Pasillo

Serves 4
Preparation time: 30 minutes

2 ancho chiles, washed and
  seeded
4 pasillo chiles, washed and
  seeded
3 tomatoes, roasted and peeled
3 cloves garlic
1 onion, sliced
6 leftover tortillas, cut in strips
¾ cup sunflower oil
2 quarts Vegetable Stock
  (page 34)
1 sprig fresh epazote, or
  1 teaspoon dried oregano
1 cup Jack cheese, chopped
  (optional)
1 ripe avocado, sliced
sea salt to taste

This variation produces a dark brown broth that is mildly spicy.

Blend the chiles, tomatoes, garlic, and onion, and strain. Heat the oil in a heavy pan, fry the tortillas until crisp, and drain. Sauté the chile purée 3 minutes in 2 tablespoons of the remaining oil. Add the vegetable stock and epazote, and simmer 15 minutes. Place the cheese and avocado in bowls, ladle the hot broth over them, and serve with chopped green onions, cilantro, salsa, and fresh lime wedges on the side.

Per serving: Calories: 309, Protein: 5 gm., Fat: 15 gm., Carbohydrates: 36 gm.

Leek and Potato Soup

Sopa de Papa con Poro

This is a popular soup in southern Mexico. It's low in fat and easy to prepare.

Serves 4
Preparation time: 15 minutes
Cooking time: 30 minutes

Sauté the leeks in the oil and butter for 5 minutes. Add the potatoes and sauté for 5 more minutes. Add the stock and simmer on low heat for 20 minutes more. Serve with a dollop of plain yogurt and a sprinkling of chives.

Per serving: Calories: 233, Protein: 5 gm., Fat: 8 gm., Carbohydrates: 36 gm.

2 leeks, well-washed and sliced
1 tablespoon olive oil
1 tablespoon butter
1 pound potatoes, chopped
1 quart vegetable stock or water
salt to taste
garnish:
1 cup low-fat plain yogurt
¼ cup chives, minced

Cactus Soup

Sopa de Nopal

Serves 4
Preparation time: 15 minutes
Cooking time: 20 minutes

The tender young leaves of the prickly pear cactus (nopal) are delicious and very nutritious.

6 tender cactus leaves, spines
  removed and chopped, or
  one 8 ounce can nopalitos
1 quart boiling salted water
⅛ teaspoon baking soda
2 whole cloves garlic
1 small onion, sliced
1 pound green tomatillos, roasted
  in a skillet
1 quart water
1 chipotle chile (optional)
½ teaspoon marjoram

Boil the cactus leaves in the salted water with the baking soda, garlic, and onion for 20 minutes. Boil in a copper pot, if you have one, or with a clean copper penny, for best results. The copper cuts the slime produced by the nopalitos when they are boiled. Drain and rinse. Roast the tomatillos in a skillet for 5 minutes, turning occasionally. Blend the tomatillos with the garlic and 1 cup of water. Strain and add the cactus leaves, the chipotle chile (only for those who like it spicy), plus 3 more cups of water. Add the marjoram, bring to a boil, and salt to taste. Serve with tortillas warmed in a dry skillet, wrapped in a cloth napkin.

Per serving: Calories: 59, Protein: 2 gm., Fat: 0 gm., Carbohydrates: 12 gm.

Variation:
2 cloves garlic, minced
1 onion, chopped
2 tomatoes, roasted, peeled, and
  seeded
2 tablespoons olive oil

Variation:
Sauté the garlic, onion, and tomatoes in the oil for 10 minutes. Add the boiled cactus, 1 quart water, a sprig of fresh epazote, and 1 chipotle chile; heat through. Salt to taste and serve.

Per serving: Calories: 114, Protein: 2 gm., Fat: 7 gm., Carbohydrates: 11 gm.

Squash Blossom Soup

Sopa de Flor De Calabaza

Throughout Mexico, the markets offer bright yellow squash blossoms, which can be prepared in a number of delicious ways. In the U.S., you will only obtain them if you grow zucchini squash in the summer. If you do, then this recipe is for you!

Sauté the corn, onion, chiles, and blossoms in the oil over low heat for 10 minutes. Add the stock, bring to a boil, and cook for 15 more minutes. Season with salt to taste. Gradually spoon the broth into the yogurt or cream, blending smooth after each addition. Serve immediately with the fresh flowers floating on top.

Per serving: Calories: 259, Protein: 8 gm., Fat: 8 gm., Carbohydrates: 37 gm.

Serves 6
Preparation time: 20 minutes
Cooking time: 25 minutes

3 cups sweet corn, cut fresh from the cob
1 onion, finely chopped
2 fresh poblano chiles, sliced in strips
2 cups squash blossoms, washed, with the stamen removed, and chopped
2 tablespoons sunflower oil
1 quart Vegetable Stock (page 34)
sea salt to taste
2 cups low-fat yogurt or sour cream
6 fresh squash blossoms, torn into strips

Calabacita Soup

Sopa de Tres Milpas

Serves 6
Preparation time: 20 minutes
Cooking time: 40 minutes

5 cloves garlic, roasted and smashed
1 red onion, sliced
1 cup sweet corn kernels
2 tablespoons sunflower or corn oil
1 quart Vegetable Stock (page 34) or water
1 sprig of fresh epazote or 2 teaspoons dried
1 pound small squash, chopped
2 cups squash blossoms, chopped (optional)
3 poblano chiles, roasted, peeled, and cut into strips

Calabacita means "little squash" and refers either to young zucchini or a round variety of small green squash similar to zucchini.

Sauté the garlic, onion, and corn in the oil. Add the stock, epazote, and squash, and simmer for 20 minutes. Add the squash blossoms and chiles, and simmer for another 15 minutes and serve.

Per serving: Calories: 173, Protein: 2 gm., Fat: 7 gm., Carbohydrates: 24 gm.

calabacitas con ajo

Creamed Poblano Soup

Caldo Largo

Poblano chiles are the mild green chiles that are stuffed with cheese and other fillings. This recipe does it great service. This may be too spicy for children, but most adults down it very enthusiastically.

Sauté the onion, garlic, and chiles in the oil for 10 minutes on medium heat. Add the stock and simmer for 15 more minutes. Add the broth gradually to the yogurt, stirring until blended after each addition. Add the salt. Heat on low for a few minutes, stirring constantly, and do not allow to boil. Distribute the cheese into six bowls, pour the hot soup over the cheese, and serve immediately.

Per serving: Calories: 324, Protein: 17 gm., Fat: 17 gm., Carbohydrates: 24 gm.

Serves 6
Preparation time: 15 minutes
Cooking time: 25 minutes

1 medium onion, sliced
4 cloves garlic, minced
6 poblano chiles, roasted, peeled, and cut in strips
1 tablespoon sunflower or sesame oil
1 quart Vegetable Stock (page 34) or water
2 cups low-fat yogurt or sour cream
2 cups Chihuahua or Monterey Jack cheese, cubed
sea salt to taste

Fresh Corn Soup

Sopa de Elote

Serves 6-8
Preparation time: 10 minutes
Cooking time: 30 minutes

3 cloves of garlic, peeled and
   chopped
1 medium onion, sliced
3 cups of sweet corn
2 cups Vegetable Stock (page 34)
2 cups low-fat milk
sea salt to taste
¼ teaspoon ground white
   pepper
⅛ teaspoon ground nutmeg

Variation:
1 poblano chile, roasted, peeled,
   and sliced

This is easy and delicious, and children love it.

Sauté the garlic, onion, and corn in a little of the vegetable stock for 10 minutes. Add the rest of the stock, and simmer for 20 minutes. Blend and add the milk. Heat on low (do not allow to boil), season with salt, pepper, and nutmeg, and serve hot.

Per serving: Calories: 129, Protein: 5 gm., Fat: 1 gm., Carbohydrates: 23 gm.

Variation:
   Add the poblano chile when sautéing. Adorn the soup with thinly sliced strips of roasted and peeled poblano chile when served.

Cold Cream of Avocado Soup

Sopa de Aguacate

My husband calls the avocado "tree butter" and uses it on bread instead of dairy butter. It is naturally so delicious that very little seasoning is required to make it savory. Use only sweet, ripe avocados for this exotic soup, testing each one before using.

Blend the pulp of the avocados with the garlic and the lime peel. Add the stock and blend 2 minutes. Add the yogurt and salt to taste, blend 1 more minute, and chill in individual dishes in the refrigerator for 45 minutes to 1 hour. Serve with tostada chips and Guadalajara Hot Sauce.

Per serving: Calories: 246, Protein: 6 gm., Fat: 13 gm., Carbohydrates: 23 gm.

Serves 6-8
Preparation time: 10 minutes, plus 1 hour chilling

3 large avocados
2 cloves garlic, roasted and smashed
grated peel of 1 lime
3 cups Vegetable Stock (page 34) or water
2 cups low-fat yogurt
finely ground sea salt to taste
Guadalajara Hot Sauce (page 143) (optional)

Cold Cream of Avocado with Tequila

Crema de Aguacate con Tequila

Serves 6-8
Preparation time: 15 minutes

1 pound ripe avocados
1 cup orange juice
3 tablespoons tequila
3 cups cold Vegetable Stock
  (page 34)
2 tablespoons fresh cilantro,
  chopped
1 fresh jalapeño chile, seeded
  and chopped
sea salt to taste
tostadas

This recipe comes from the state of Jalisco, where tequila is produced. The taste of the tequila is very subtle; in combination with the orange juice and cilantro, it freshens and enhances the delicate flavor of the avocado.

Blend the avocados with the orange juice. Gradually add the remaining ingredients, and continue blending until smooth. Serve immediately, with tostadas on the side.

Per serving: Calories: 161, Protein: 2 gm., Fat: 8 gm., Carbohydrates: 17 gm.

Black Bean Soup

Sopa de Frijol Negro

This is the best black bean soup I've ever tried. The inspiration comes from Greens Restaurant in San Francisco, but it has undergone some changes at La Casa del Pan.

Soak the beans in enough water to cover overnight, then drain, and rinse. Boil vigorously in the 3 quarts water for 2 hours, adding water as necessary to keep the broth soupy. Add the epazote, bay leaves, garlic, salt, chiles, cumin, and oregano, and boil for another hour until the beans are very tender. Add the cilantro and tomato, and cook for 15 more minutes, adding water if necessary. The broth should be plentiful and thick. Serve with a spoonful of garnish in the center of the bowl and warm tortillas wrapped in a cloth napkin.

Per serving: Calories: 259, Protein: 14 gm., Fat: 1 gm., Carbohydrates: 48 gm.

Serves 6-8
Preparation time: 15 minutes
Cooking time: 3 hours

2 cups dried black beans, cleaned
3 quarts water
1 sprig fresh epazote
2 bay leaves
6 cloves whole garlic
1 teaspoon sea salt
2 ancho chiles
2 chipotle chiles
1 teaspoon powdered chile pequín
1 tablespoon cumin powder
1 tablespoon dried oregano
⅓ cup cilantro leaves, chopped
1 pound tomatoes, peeled, seeded, and chopped
garnish:
2 green onions, chopped
2 green jalapeño chiles, chopped
1 large tomato, peeled, seeded, and chopped
½ cup yogurt or sour cream (optional)

Garlic Soup

Sopa de Ajo

Serves 6
Preparation time: 10 minutes
Cooking time: 25 minutes

2 Tablespoons cold pressed olive
   oil
2 large heads of garlic, unpeeled
6 cups Vegetable Stock (page 34)
   or water
2 cups tomatoes, coarsely
   chopped
2 teaspoons thyme
1 teaspoon oregano
1 bay leaf
sea salt
freshly ground black pepper
½ cup sherry
seasoned croutons

This soup is as nutritious as it is delicious. Garlic is high in germanium, an element proven to oxygenate the blood and fortify the immune system. The garlic becomes sweet as it cooks.

Heat the oil in a medium-sized saucepan. Add the whole heads of garlic, and sauté over moderate heat, smashing the garlic with a large spoon. Add the stock, tomatoes, thyme, oregano, and bay leaf, and simmer for 20 minutes. Press through a strainer. Season with salt, pepper, and sherry. Heat until the soup barely starts to simmer, and serve in individual bowls. Adorn with seasoned croutons. This soup is traditionally served over raw egg, but cubed tofu could be substituted.

Per serving: Calories: 213, Protein: 3 gm., Fat: 9 gm., Carbohydrates: 25 gm.

Vegetarian Pozole

Pozole Vegetariano

Pozole is originally from the state of Jalisco. It is served throughout Mexico on the eve of the sixteenth of September during the Independence Day Celebration. Traditionally, it is made with pork and chicken. I am grateful to Nelva Ugarte who taught me this recipe when we prepared it for the Independence Celebration at La Casa del Pan in Mexico City. The combination of oyster mushrooms, pimentos, and hominy is memorable. When it is served with all its garnishes, this is a very colorful dish. This one-dish meal is recommended for a party of 20 people! (If you are serving fewer than 6 people, divide the ingredients by 4.)

Put the hominy on to cook with the water, garlic, onion, pimentos, and mushrooms for 2 hours.

Add the oregano, salt to taste, and cook for another hour.

Meanwhile, prepare the garnishes, arranging them on the table in serving dishes. Serve the pozole in individual bowls, and invite your dinner guests to apply their own garnishes.

VIVA MEXICO!

Per serving (soup only): Calories: 101, Protein: 3 gm., Fat: 0 gm., Carbohydrates: 22 gm.

Per serving (with garnish): Calories: 158, Protein: 4 gm., Fat: 2 gm., Carbohydrates: 31 gm.

Serves 20
Preparation time: 20 minutes
Cooking time: 3 hours

4 pounds cooked hominy, or
  2 pounds dried hominy corn
8 quarts water (add more as
  needed)
1 whole head of garlic
1 whole onion, sliced
2 pounds raw red pimentos, cut
  into strips
2 pounds oyster mushrooms, cut
  into strips
2 teaspoons oregano, dried
sea salt to taste
garnishes:
2 large red onions, chopped
1 pound radishes, sliced
1 head of iceberg lettuce,
  shredded
60 whole tostadas, or 4 large bags
  of tostada chips
½ cup dried oregano
½ cup powdered chile pequín
10 limes, cut into wedges

Shipwrecked Cactus Soup

Nopalitos Navegantes

Serves 6
Preparation time: 20 minutes
Cooking time: 15 minutes

The name in Spanish for this soup is "nopalitos navegantes," which means "sailing nopalitos," but my kids call them "nopalitos naúfragos," which means "shipwrecked nopalitos." Young, tender cactus leaves from the prickly pear cactus or nopalitos are one of my favorite foods, and they are very nutritious.

6 tender nopalitos (cactus leaves), chopped, or one 8-ounce can
1 clove garlic, roasted and smashed
1 medium onion, sliced
1 quart well salted boiling water
thin pinch of baking soda
1 pound tomatoes
1 huajillo chile
1 quart water
6 eggs
sea salt to taste

Boil the nopalitos, garlic, and onion in the salted water with baking soda for 20 minutes. Meanwhile, roast the tomatoes and the chile in a heavy skillet on medium heat until scorched on all sides. Blend with 1 cup of the water, and strain through a medium-mesh strainer. Add the rest of the water, and heat. Rinse the cooked nopalitos in fresh water, and drain. Add the nopalitos to the tomato huajillo broth, and heat to a boil, adding salt if desired. Lower the heat. Crack open 6 eggs and add them, one at a time, to the simmering broth. Cook until the eggs are firm, and serve.

Per serving: Calories: 121, Protein: 8 gm., Fat: 6 gm., Carbohydrates: 9 gm.

Garden Mushroom Soup

Sopa de Hongos Jardinera

This is an aromatic and hearty soup which makes a meal when served with a salad and whole grain bread. This original recipe is from La Casa del Pan.

Sauté the garlic, onion, mushrooms, and chiles in olive oil over medium heat, stirring, for 5 minutes. Add the tomatoes, water, chayotes, zucchini, carrots, and chard, and season with thyme and salt. Simmer for 15 more minutes, remove the chiles, and serve.

Per serving: Calories: 196, Protein: 4 gm., Fat: 9 gm., Carbohydrates: 24 gm.

Serves 6
Preparation time: 20 minutes
Cooking time: 15 minutes

10 cloves garlic, roasted and squeezed out of their jackets
1 onion, sliced
1 pound oyster mushrooms or other mushrooms
3 whole huajillo chiles
¼ cup olive oil
2 cups puréed tomatoes
2 cups water
½ pound chayotes, cubed
½ pound zucchini, cubed
½ pound carrots, cubed
½ pound Swiss chard, chopped
2 teaspoons dried thyme
sea salt to taste

chayotes

Cilantro Soup with Tostadas

Sopa de Cilantro

Serves 6
Preparation time: 20 minutes
Cooking time: 30 minutes

1 pound zucchini, cubed
1 cup salted water
3 tablespoons butter or vegetable
   oil
1 medium onion, minced
1 jalapeño chile
1 cup fresh cilantro, washed,
   chopped, and compacted
5 cups Vegetable Stock (page 34)
   or water
½ teaspoon fine sea salt
garnish:
1 cup panela or other fresh
   cheese, cubed
½ cup low-fat yogurt or sour
cream
⅔ cup tortilla chips, broken

Cilantro is also known as Chinese parsley. It has a very pungent flavor, agreeable to many, but not to all. One of our customers claims that this is due to one's genetic makeup. What tastes like an aromatic herb to some, tastes like detergent to others. I like cilantro, and this soup is one of my favorites. It is from Mexico City.

Cook the zucchini in 1 cup salted water, covered, for 15 minutes. Meanwhile, melt the butter in a 2-quart pan over medium heat, and sauté the onion for 5 minutes. Add the whole chile and sauté 5 more minutes. When the zucchini is tender, blend with the cilantro until smooth, gradually adding the broth in which the zucchini was cooked and the vegetable stock. You will need to blend this in two or three batches. Add to the onion and chile, and bring to a boil. Lower the heat and simmer for 10 minutes. Remove the chile, and season with salt. Place some of the cheese in each bowl, ladle the hot soup on top, and garnish with yogurt and tortilla chips.

Per serving: Calories: 266, Protein: 9 gm., Fat: 17 gm., Carbohydrates: 20 gm.

Cheese Soup

Sopa de Queso

This soup comes originally from the state of Sonora in northern Mexico. The cheese traditionally used is called Chihuahua and is frequently made by Mennonites who have lived in Chihuahua since the 19th century. It resembles a good Jack cheese or a mild white cheddar. Either will make a good substitute in this recipe.

Serves 6
Preparation time: 25 minutes
Cooking time: 15 minutes

Melt the butter in a 2-quart saucepan, add the onion and sauté over medium heat, stirring, for 5 minutes. Add the pimento and chile, sauté 5 more minutes, and remove from the heat. Sprinkle the flour over the vegetables, and stir to combine. Gradually, one tablespoon at a time at first, add the water, stirring to combine. Return to the heat, stirring while the broth thickens. Add the milk, salt, and chile, correct the seasoning, and heat through. Distribute the cheese in six bowls, and pour the soup over the cheese.

Per serving: Calories: 198, Protein: 12 gm., Fat: 9 gm., Carbohydrates: 14 gm.

2 tablespoons butter
1 small onion, minced
1 large red pimento pepper, chopped
1 large poblano chile, roasted, peeled, deveined, and chopped
2 tablespoons flour
4 cups water
2 cups evaporated skim milk
½ teaspoon salt
pinch of ground chile pequín
1 cup Chihuahua cheese, grated

Fava Bean Soup with Cactus

Sopa de Habas Con Nopal

Serves 6-8
Preparation time: 20 minutes
Cooking Time: 2 hours

1 pound fresh fava beans, or
½ pound dried
2 quarts water
½ pound fresh nopalitos (young
cactus leaves), cut in ½-inch
squares
1 medium onion, sliced
1 tablespoon sea salt (for cooking
the nopales)
2 teaspoons baking soda
1 quart water
1 large onion, chopped
5 cloves garlic, peeled and
chopped
¼ cup sunflower or sesame oil
½ pound tomatoes, peeled,
seeded, and chopped
½ cup fresh cilantro leaves,
chopped
2 tablespoons fresh epazote
leaves, chopped
sea salt to taste

This is La Casa del Pan's version of the soup served at Sak's Vegetarian Restaurant in Mexico City, which the owner Isaac Bejar, calls "Sopa Campesina."

Boil the fava beans in 2 quarts water until tender. If they are dried, soak them overnight, drain and cook in fresh water. (This will shorten the cooking time.) Boil the nopales with the sliced onion, salt, and soda in 1 quart water for 30 minutes, drain, and rinse well. Use three changes of water if necessary, to eliminate the slime.

In a 2-quart saucepan over medium heat, sauté the chopped onion and garlic in the oil for 10 minutes, stirring occasionally. Add the tomatoes, cilantro, epazote, and half of the fava beans, and continue to cook for 10 minutes, stirring occasionally. Blend the rest of the fava beans with some of the water in which they were cooked, and add to the pot with the rest of the water. Cook for 10 minutes and add the salt.

Per serving: Calories: 177, Protein: 5 gm., Fat: 8 gm., Carbohydrates: 21 gm..

Cream of Chayote

Crema de Chayote

This simple soup is rich, and the pecan croutons give it an interesting contrast in texture.

Serves 4-6
Preparation time: 20 minutes
Cooking time: 35 minutes

Boil the chayotes in 1 quart water with 1 tablespoon salt for 20 minutes. Peel the chayotes and cut them in half. Remove the smooth seeds and reserve. Remove the fibrous seed casings around the seeds, and discard. Blend the chayotes and their smooth inner seeds with a little of the water in which they were boiled. In a 2-quart saucepan, melt the butter or oil, and sauté the onion for 10 minutes, stirring occasionally. Add the chayote puree and the rest of the water in which the chayotes were boiled. Bring to a boil, stirring occasionally. Lower the heat to a simmer. Just before serving the soup, stir in the sour cream, white pepper, and nutmeg. Ladle into individual bowls, and sprinkle the croutons on top.

To prepare the croutons, melt the butter in a skillet. Add the bread cubes, pecans, black pepper, and salt, and toss to cover the bread cubes well. Bake in a slow oven (300°F) for 20 minutes.

Per serving: Calories: 352, Protein: 5 gm., Fat: 28 gm., Carbohydrates: 20 gm.

6 chayotes
1 quart water
1 tablespoon sea salt
¼ cup butter or vegetable oil
1 medium onion, finely chopped
**¾ cup sour cream or plain
  yogurt (optional)**
¼ teaspoon white pepper
grating of nutmeg
croutons:
¼ cup butter or vegetable oil
1 cup bread, cubed
**¼ cup pecans, ground in a
  blender or food processor**
freshly ground black pepper
**¼ teaspoon finely ground sea
  salt**

Lentil Soup

Sopa de Lenteja

Serves 6-8
Preparation time: 15 minutes
Cooking time: 2 hours

2 tablespoons olive oil
8 cloves garlic, peeled and
   chopped
1 pound tomatoes, peeled and
   chopped
6 cups water
1 pound lentils
1½ teaspoons sea salt
2 chipotle chiles
½ pound Swiss chard

The smoked chipotle chile gives this soup a spicy, barbecued flavor. Sometimes we add diced potatoes or carrots with the chard.

Heat the oil in a 4-quart saucepan over medium heat. Sauté the garlic, stirring occasionally, for 5 minutes. Add the tomatoes and sauté another 10 minutes. Add the water and lentils, bring to a boil, cover, and cook over low heat until the lentils are tender, about 1½ hours. Add the salt, the chiles, and Swiss chard, and cook 15 more minutes before serving. Warn your dinner guests about the chiles!

Per serving: Calories: 138, Protein: 6 gm., Fat: 4 gm., Carbohydrates: 19 gm.

Lime Soup

Sopa de Lima

This fragrant and savory soup is an adaptation of the traditional recipe from the Yucatan Peninsula. The characteristic flavor of this soup comes from the limas, which are neither limes nor lemons. They look like large pale limes. If you cannot get limas, limes make an agreeable substitute.

To make the vegetable broth, boil the water in a 6-quart pot with the garlic, quartered onions, cilantro, epazote, and salt for 20 minutes. Meanwhile, in a dry skillet over medium heat, toast the cumin, cinnamon, allspice, cloves, and oregano for 3 minutes. Grind the spices in a blender with ½ cup water, strain, and reserve the liquid.

Heat the oil in a 6-quart pot over moderate heat, and sauté the finely chopped onions for 2 minutes. Add the pimentos, and cook 3 minutes. Next, add the tomatoes, cover, and cook over low heat for 10 minutes. Strain the vegetable broth and pour it over the vegetables. Add the strained spice liquid.

When the soup starts to boil, add the sherry, lime juice, and lime slices, reserving the lime wedges. Cover the soup and cook over medium heat for 10 more minutes. Meanwhile, fry the tortilla strips in the oil until crisp, and drain before placing in individual bowls. Arrange the avocado slices on top of the tortilla strips, and ladle the hot soup over them. Serve with lime wedges.

Per serving: Calories: 267, Protein: 5 gm., Fat: 12 gm., Carbohydrates: 32 gm.

Serves 10
Preparation time: 30 minutes
Cooking time: 35 minutes

5 quarts water
10 cloves garlic, unpeeled
1½ onions, quartered
10 sprigs cilantro
2 sprigs epazote or parsley
2 tablespoons coarse sea salt
2 teaspoons ground cumin
3 sticks cinnamon, about 2 inches long
6 whole seeds allspice, or 1 teaspoon ground
3 whole cloves
3 teaspoons oregano, dried
1 tablespoon vegetable oil
1½ red onions, finely chopped
1½ green pimentos or green bell peppers, finely chopped
2 cups tomatoes, peeled and chopped
¼ cup dry sherry
12 limas (see page 13) or limes, 2 cut in thin slices, 5 cut in wedges, and 5 squeezed for juice
10 tortillas, cut into thin strips
2 tablespoons vegetable oil
3 avocados, peeled and sliced

Pasta Soup

Sopa de Pasta

Serves 6
Preparation time: 15 minutes
Cooking time: 20 minutes

1½ tablespoons sunflower oil
½ pound vermicelli (or flat
  noodles, macaroni, shells, etc.)
6 Italian tomatoes, coarsely
  chopped
½ cup onion, coarsely chopped
2 cloves garlic, peeled
2 quarts hot Vegetable Stock
  (page 34) or water
garnish:
3 small chipotle chiles, halved
  and slightly roasted (optional)
2 avocados, sliced
dollop of sour cream or plain,
  natural yogurt (optional)

The secret of Mexican sopa de pasta is the proper browning of the pasta in oil, as explained below. Any kind of pasta appropriate for soup may be used. Vermicelli is suggested here.

Heat the oil in a 3-quart saucepan, add the pasta, and stir until it begins to brown, about 10 minutes. Remove from the heat and drain off the excess oil. Blend the tomatoes with the onion and garlic. Put the tomato mixture through a strainer, return the pasta to the heat, and add the tomatoes to the pasta. Cook until it begins to boil, and add the hot vegetable stock or water. Cook over medium heat until the pasta is tender, about 10 minutes. Serve in 6 bowls and decorate each bowl with ½ chile, avocado slices, and a dollop of sour cream or yogurt, if desired.

Per serving: Calories: 203, Protein: 3 gm., Fat: 12 gm., Carbohydrates: 20 gm.

Chipilín Soup with Masa Balls

Sopa de Chipilín con Bola

This soup from the southern state of Chiapas has pre-Hispanic origins. The cheese and cream were probably added in this century. Chipilín is a mild-flavored green with small leaves. You can use watercress, Swiss chard, or spinach as substitutes. Fresh tortilla dough can be obtained at a tortilla factory, or it can be prepared from dry masa harina, available in the Mexican foods section of most supermarkets.

Boil the onions, chiles, and corn in the vegetable stock until the corn is tender, about 20 minutes. Meanwhile, to make the masa balls, add the oil, salt, and cheese to the tortilla dough, mix well, and form marble-sized balls by rolling bits of dough between the palms of your hands. Place on a platter.

Season the soup with salt, and add the chipilín. Dissolve the corn flour in a little water, and add to the soup. Lower the heat to a simmer, and drop the masa balls into the broth, one at a time. Cook for 20 more minutes, and serve with fresh chipilín leaves, yogurt, and cubed cheese on the side.

Per serving: Calories: 232, Protein: 6 gm., Fat: 13 gm., Carbohydrates: 23 gm.

Serves 8-10
Preparation time: 40 minutes

soup:
1 bunch green onions, cut lengthwise in strips
3 medium onions, sliced
2 fresh jalapeño chiles or other fresh chiles
3 quarts Vegetable Stock (page 34) or water
2 cups fresh corn kernels
1 teaspoon sea salt, or to taste
2 cups fresh chipilín, watercress, Swiss chard, or spinach, chopped
¼ cup corn flour
masa balls:
½ cup sunflower oil
sea salt to taste
1 cup farmer's cheese, crumbled
1 pound fresh tortilla dough
garnishes: (optional)
fresh chipilín, watercress, Swiss chard, or spinach
1 cup low-fat yogurt or sour cream
1½ cups farmer's cheese, cubed

Salads

Ensaladas

Jícama Peanut Salad

Ensalada de Jícama con Cacahuate

Serves 4
Preparation time: 15 minutes

2 medium jícamas, peeled and
   sliced
1 bell pepper, cut in strips
2 tablespoons roasted peanuts
1 tablespoon fresh parsley or
   cilantro, chopped
¼ to ½ teaspoon ground chile
   pequín
juice of 2 limes
½ teaspoon sea salt

Jícama is a mild, juicy, crispy root, which is light in color with a light brown skin. It comes in all sizes and is in season in the winter months. Water chestnuts may be used as a substitute in many recipes.

Arrange the jícama on a platter with the bell pepper strips and the peanuts on top. Sprinkle with the parsley, chile pequín, lime juice, and sea salt, and serve. It's light, delicious, and different!

Per serving: Calories: 65, Protein: 1 gm., Fat: 2 gm., Carbohydrates: 10 gm.

Jícama-Orange Salad

Ensalada de Jícama con Naranja

Serves 6
Preparation time: 15 minutes

8 oranges, peeled and sliced
1 large red onion, finely chopped
2 cups jícama, peeled and
   chopped into ½-inch cubes
1 cup cilantro, chopped
   (optional)
½ teaspoon powdered chile
   pequín
½ teaspoon sea salt, or to taste

Here is a variation of how Mexicans traditionally eat jícama, sprinkled with fresh lime juice, salt, and powdered, dried chile.

Arrange half of the oranges on a platter. Toss the onion, jícama, cilantro, chile, and salt together, and layer half of this mixture over the orange slices. Make another layer with the rest of the oranges. Place the rest of the jícama mixture on top. Decorate with cilantro leaves and thin slices of red onion.

Per serving: Calories: 117, Protein: 2 gm., Fat: 0 gm., Carbohydrates: 27 gm.

Jícama Watercress Salad

Ensalada de Jícama con Berros

Jícama and watercress are abundant in Mexican markets. In this recipe, they are combined with avocados and red pimentos and served with a mustard-nut dressing.

Roast the pecans in a dry skillet over medium heat for 3 minutes. To make the dressing, blend the pecans, lime juice, cilantro, watercress, and mustard. With the blender still turned on, slowly add the oil until thick and creamy. In a bowl, combine the jícama, pimento, and watercress. Make a bed of lettuce on the serving plates. Place the jícama mixture on top of the lettuce, and adorn with the avocado cubes, cilantro leaves, dressing and black pepper.

Per serving: Calories: 270, Protein: 2 gm., Fat: 17 gm., Carbohydrates: 26 gm.

Serves 5
Preparation time: 25 minutes

dressing:
2 tablespoons pecans
¼ cup lime juice
2 tablespoons fresh cilantro
2 tablespoons watercress
1 teaspoon Dijon mustard
¼ cup olive oil
salad:
1 pound jícama, peeled and julienned
1 red pimento, seeded and chopped
2 cups watercress, destemmed and chopped
whole red lettuce leaves
1 avocado, peeled and cut into cubes and sprinkled with lime juice
¼ cup fresh cilantro leaves
freshly grated black pepper to taste

Jícama Chipotle Salad

Ensalada de Jícama con Chipotle

Serves 4
Preparation time: 20 minutes
Chilling time: 4 hours

2 medium jícamas, peeled and
diced
1 large carrot, peeled, diced, and
parboiled
1 medium zucchini, washed and
chopped
1-2 chipotle chiles, chopped with
their liquid (they are hot)
2 green onions with greens,
chopped
4 cloves garlic, chopped
1 bay leaf
¼ teaspoon freshly ground
black pepper
3 tablespoons apple cider vinegar
¼ cup water
¼ cup olive oil
2 teaspoons fresh cilantro,
chopped
1 teaspoon dried oregano
½ teaspoon salt, or to taste

This is my favorite salad, thanks to Mimi Laughlin who was so generous to share it. Besides being an outstanding vegetarian cook, Mimi has captured the surreal essence of Chiapas in her excellent short stories about its people.

Combine the jícama, carrot, and zucchini. In a separate bowl, combine the rest of the ingredients, and whisk. Pour over the jícama mixture, toss, and refrigerate. Marinate for at least 4 hours, tossing occasionally. Serve over a crisp bed of lettuce.

Per serving: Calories: 205, Protein: 2 gm., Fat: 13 gm., Carbohydrates: 20 gm.

Sweet Basil Vinaigrette

Aderezo de Albahaca

Yield: 1 cup
Preparation time: 10 minutes

Combine all the ingredients together in a blender.

Per 2 tablespoons: Calories: 30, Protein: 0 gm., Fat: 2 gm., Carbohydrates: 2 gm.

¼ cup olive oil
¼ cup wine vinegar
¼ cup water
2 cloves fresh garlic
¼ cup fresh sweet basil, washed and coarsely chopped
½ teaspoon brown sugar
¼ teaspoon sea salt
⅛ teaspoon freshly ground black pepper

Lime Salad Dressing

Aderezo de Limón

Serves 8 people
Preparation time: 10 minutes

This can be made in the blender if you don't have a molcajeta, but I recommend obtaining one whenever possible, since the physical process of combining the ingredients between smooth stones brings better results than a blender. The molcajeta is basic for numerous Mexican sauces.

Smash or blend the garlic with the peppercorns, and gradually add the lime juice. Add the olive oil a little at a time, and then the salt, sugar, and water, and strain. Shake just before pouring over the salad.

Per serving: Calories: 49, Protein: 0 gm., Fat: 5 gm., Carbohydrates: 1 gm.

3 fat cloves of fresh garlic
10 peppercorns
juice of 2 limes
3 tablespoons olive oil
¼ teaspoon sea salt
½ teaspoon brown sugar
1½ teaspoons spring water

Tossed Salad from La Casa del Pan

Ensalada de La Casa

Serves 4-6
Preparation time: 15 minutes

This is the salad we serve every day. It is based on organic, home-grown ingredients provided by our garden and those of our friends. A variety of interesting greens and a sweet basil vinaigrette is the essence of this salad, which varies somewhat from day to day.

1 quart mixed salad greens (butter lettuce, red lettuce, oak lettuce, romaine lettuce, arugula, mustard greens, endive, frigée, etc.) thoroughly washed and dried

3 small red tomatoes, washed and thinly sliced

2 avocados, peeled and sliced

¼ cup pickled julienned beets or carrots

3 scallions with greens, chopped

Sweet Basil Vinaigrette (page 63)

Toss the salad greens together, and place in individual bowls. Adorn with the tomatoes, avocado slices, beets, and scallions. Serve with Sweet Basil Vinaigrette.

Per serving: Calories: 164, Protein: 3 gm., Fat: 10 gm., Carbohydrates: 16 gm.

Nopalito Cactus Salad

Ensalada de Nopalito

In the marketplace in Xochimilco (Mexico City), vendors prepare this salad in their stalls and dish it up to their clients to carry home in plastic bags.

Serves 4-6
Preparation time: 30 minutes

Bring the water and salt to a boil in a 4-quart saucepan. Add the nopalitos, garlic, and onion, boil for 30 minutes, and drain. Cover with cold water, and drain again. Repeat twice more, if necessary, to remove any slime the nopalitos may have. Add the vinegar, oil, onion, tomatoes, cilantro, chiles, and salt, and toss to combine. Decorate with avocado slices and fresh cheese cubes, if desired.

Per serving: Calories: 403, Protein: 3 gm., Fat: 25 gm., Carbohydrates: 37 gm.

2 quarts water
1 tablespoon sea salt
10 to 15 young nopalito pads, despined and cut into 1-inch strips
4 whole cloves garlic
1 medium onion, sliced
½ cup apple cider vinegar
½ cup sesame or sunflower oil
1 red onion, thinly sliced
6 Italian tomatoes, chopped
1 cup cilantro, chopped
2 jalapeño chiles, deveined, seeded, and chopped
sea salt to taste
1 avocado, sliced
1 cup farmer's cheese or other fresh cheese, cubed (optional)

Cilantro Dressing

Aderezo de Cilantro

Serves 10
Preparation time: 10 minutes

½ cup mayonnaise
¼ cup fresh cilantro, washed
  and coarsely chopped
2 tablespoons olive oil
2 tablespoons lime juice
2 cloves garlic
2 tablespoons white wine
  vinegar
salt and pepper to taste

Paola de María y Campos, a special helper and young friend of mine and my kids, showed me how to make this hit dressing

Combine all the ingredients in a blender. Serve over tossed salad.

Per serving: Calories: 62, Protein: 0 gm., Fat: 6 gm., Carbohydrates: 2 gm.

Herbed Zucchini Salad

Ensalada de Calabacita

This salad is refreshing and intriguing for its flavors and originality. Thanks to Mimi Laughlin.

To prepare the marinade, mix the lime, garlic, honey, salt, chile, and mint. Gradually add the oil, while beating with a whisk, or mix in a blender.

Boil the zucchini for 2½ minutes, and drain. Arrange the zucchini in a serving platter. Add the strips of chiles, scallions, cream cheese, mint, and cilantro. Season with salt and cover with the marinade. Mix well and refrigerate. Mix again every half hour until serving time. Serve on individual plates over shredded lettuce, and garnish with avocado slices, fresh mint leaves, and lime wedges.

Per serving: Calories: 292, Protein: 5 gm., Fat: 23 gm., Carbohydrates: 15 gm.

Serves 5-6
Preparation time: 30 minutes

marinade:
⅓ cup fresh lime or lemon juice
4 cloves garlic, peeled and chopped
1 teaspoon honey
½ teaspoon salt
½ teaspoon ground chile pequín
3 tablespoons fresh mint, chopped
¼ cup extra virgin olive oil

salad:
5 medium zucchini, sliced
4 jalapeño or serrano chiles, cut in strips
6 scallions, chopped
4 ounces cream cheese, cut in strips
2 tablespoons, fresh mint leaves, chopped
2 tablespoons cilantro, chopped
½ teaspoon salt

garnish:
1 head of lettuce, shredded
1 large avocado, sliced
2 tablespoons fresh mint, chopped
3 limes, cut in wedges

Cabbage Salad with Fresh Mexican Salsa

Ensalada de Col a La Mexicana

Serves 4-6
Preparation time: 15 minutes

1 small cabbage (4 cups), finely
  shredded
½ pound tomatoes, chopped
6 scallions with greens, chopped
½ cup cilantro, chopped
1 small jalapeño chile, chopped
juice of one lime
1 tablespoon olive oil
1 teaspoon wine vinegar
salt to taste

This salad makes a good companion to the Masa Patties from Piedras Negras (page 134).

Toss all the ingredients together, and serve.

Per serving: Calories: 52, Protein: 1 gm., Fat: 2 gm., Carbohydrates: 6 gm.

Watercress Sesame with Mustard Dressing

Ensalada de Berros y Ajonjolé con Mostaza

This is a spicy salad, high in vitamin C (from the watercress) and calcium (from the sesame seeds).

Combine the dressing ingredients in a blender, and toss with the watercress, scallions, and sesame seeds just before serving.

Per serving: Calories: 84, Protein: 1 gm., Fat: 8 gm., Carbohydrates: 2 gm.

Serves 6
Preparation time: 15 minutes

3 cups watercress, well-washed and cut into 3-inch pieces
½ cup scallions with greens, chopped
¼ cup sesame seeds, toasted
dressing:
1 tablespoon Dijon mustard
2 tablespoons olive oil
3 tablespoons white wine vinegar
½ teaspoon sea salt

Spinach with Orange Salad

Ensalada de Espinaca con Naranja

Oranges are abundant in Mexico all year round. In winter you can buy them in 50-pound bags on street corners in Mexico City. Make this recipe with fresh squeezed orange juice to get the full effect.

Mix the dressing with a whisk, and toss with the spinach, onion, and sunflower seeds just before serving.

Per serving: Calories: 111, Protein: 4 gm., Fat: 6 gm., Carbohydrates: 10 gm.

Serves 4
Preparation time: 15 minutes

4 cups fresh spinach, chopped
1 small red onion, thinly sliced
⅓ cup sunflower seeds
dressing:
⅔ cup orange juice
1 tablespoon soy sauce

Spinach Watercress Salad

Ensalada de Berros con Espinaca

Serves 4
Preparation time: 20 minutes

Make this with the freshest ingredients. Our friends George and Jane Collier, anthropologists from Stanford University who first brought us to Chiapas in 1970, approved this recipe while visiting us in San Cristobal.

1 bunch of spinach, washed and torn into bite-size pieces
1 bunch of watercress, well washed and cut into 2-inch pieces
1 avocado, sliced
1 tablespoon toasted sesame seeds
dressing:
3 cloves garlic, peeled and crushed
¼ cup olive oil
juice of 2 limes
1 teaspoon sugar
1 teaspoon salt
½ teaspoon pepper
½ teaspoon dill weed
¼ cup water

Toss the spinach and watercress together, and adorn with the avocado slices and sesame seeds. Blend the dressing ingredients and add just before serving.

Per serving: Calories: 235, Protein: 2 gm., Fat: 20 gm., Carbohydrates: 10 gm.

Avocado Carrot with Garlic Salad

Ensalada de Aguacate con Zanahoria

Angela Cuevas served this delicious salad to us in her homey, aromatic kitchen in San Cristobal at the onset of an unforgettable meal.

Serves 6
Preparation time: 15 minutes

Combine all the ingredients, toss, and let stand for ½ hour before serving. Toss again just before serving.

Per serving: Calories: 281, Protein: 2 gm., Fat: 21 gm., Carbohydrates: 20 gm.

8 cloves garlic, peeled and mashed
3 cups carrot, grated
3 ripe avocados, chopped
¼ cup olive oil
¼ cup lime juice
sea salt to taste
freshly ground black pepper

Shredded Lettuce with Lime

Ensalada de Lecluega con Limón

This salad is beautiful for its simplicity. Fresh lime juice is essential.

Serves 6-8
Preparation time: 10 minutes

Toss the lettuce with ⅔ of the lime juice and salt. Arrange the tomatoes, onion, and avocado on the lettuce, pour the rest of the lime juice over the top, and add a grinding of fresh black pepper.

Per serving: Calories: 72, Protein: 1 gm., Fat: 4 gm., Carbohydrates: 8 gm.

1 iceberg lettuce, finely shredded
juice of 3 limes
¼ teaspoon sea salt
3 Italian tomatoes, thinly sliced
1 small red onion, thinly sliced
1 avocado, sliced
freshly ground black pepper

Huitlacoche-Stuffed Avocados from Puebla

Aguacates Rellenos de Huitlacoche

Serves 8
Preparation time: 35 minutes

This unusual recipe is a delicious way to prepare huitlacoche. This Aztec delicacy is still eaten throughout the central Mexican plateau, encompassing Puebla and the Valley of Mexico. American farmers throw away this delicious mushroom, which they call corn smut. If you can't find it fresh or canned in your area, you can substitute the readily available French button mushrooms.

4 large ripe avocados
¼ cup white wine vinegar
juice of 1 lime
½ cup olive oil
sea salt to taste
freshly ground black pepper
filling:
2 tablespoons oil
1 medium onion, finely chopped
6 cloves garlic, mashed
1 pound fresh huitlacoche or
   mushrooms
3 tablespoons fresh epazote or
   parsley, chopped
2 fresh green chiles, finely
   chopped
sea salt to taste
garnish:
8 large lettuce leaves, washed,
   dried, and chilled

Cut the avocados in half, scoop out the pulp in strips, and reserve the empty shells. Place the strips of avocado on a platter. Blend the vinegar, lime juice, olive oil, salt, and pepper, pour over the avocados, and chill.

Heat the oil in a skillet, and sauté the onion and garlic for 5 minutes. Add the huitlacoche, epazote, and chile, cook for 10 minutes, and season with the salt. Cook on low for 15 more minutes, turn off the heat, and allow to cool. Fill the avocado shells with the filling, place on lettuce leaves, and serve.

Per serving: Calories: 355, Protein: 3 gm., Fat: 28 gm., Carbohydrates: 19 gm.

Ron's Potato Salad

Ensalada de Papa

This recipe is very popular. It's best to chill it for an hour before serving.

Cut the potatoes into 1-inch cubes. Combine with the scallions, chile, dill weed, dill pickles, pickle brine, salt, and pepper, and allow to marinate 3-4 hours in the refrigerator or overnight, if possible. Stir occasionally. After marinating, chop 5 of the hard-boiled eggs, and combine with the celery, oil, mustard, and yogurt, and mix well. Decorate with slices of the sixth egg and paprika.

Per serving: Calories: 270, Protein: 9 gm., Fat: 12 gm., Carbohydrates: 31 gm.

Serves 6 hungry people
Preparation time: 30 minutes

6 medium white or 12 small red potatoes, boiled until barely soft
6 scallions with greens, chopped
1 chipotle chile, minced
1½ teaspoons crushed dill weed
2 whole dill pickles, chopped
3 tablespoons dill pickle brine
2 teaspoons salt
½ teaspoon freshly ground black pepper
6 eggs, hard-boiled and peeled
3 celery ribs, chopped
2 tablespoons olive oil
¼ cup Dijon mustard
½ cup low-fat yogurt
paprika

Pickled Garbanzo Salad

Ensalada de Garbanzo

Serves 5-6
Preparation time: 20 minutes
Soaking time: 12 hours
Cooking time: 1-3 hours

½ pound dried garbanzo beans
1 quart water
4 cloves garlic
1 teaspoon sea salt
4 scallions with greens, chopped
3 tablespoons olive oil
2 teaspoons fresh gingerroot,
** peeled and grated**
3 tablespoons fresh cilantro
** leaves, chopped**
1 green jalapeño chile, chopped
1 red pimento pepper, seeded
** and chopped**
¼ teaspoon powdered chile
** pequín**
1 teaspoon fine sea salt
¼ teaspoon freshly ground black
** pepper**
2 tablespoons honey

The combination of the ginger and garbanzo in this salad is an effective digestive aid. The addition of cilantro, lime, and chile makes this a very refreshing salad.

Soak the garbanzo beans in enough water to cover overnight, then drain, and rinse. In the morning, boil the beans in 1 quart water with the garlic and until tender, from 1-3 hours. Add the salt when the beans are almost soft. Strain off the water and combine the garbanzo beans with the rest of the ingredients, tossing until well mixed. Chill for ½ hour before serving.

Per serving: Calories: 165, Protein: 3 gm., Fat: 8 gm., Carbohydrates: 20 gm.

Raw Vegetable Salad

This salad is high in fiber and contains broccoli and cabbage which are reported to have cancer-preventative qualities.

Combine the cabbage, carrots, squash, broccoli, pimento, and onion. Prepare the dressing in a bottle with a tight-fitting lid and shake vigorously to mix. Pour the dressing over the vegetables and toss to combine. Allow to marinate 1 hour, tossing occasionally. Before serving, mix the cucumbers and sprouts in with the rest of the vegetables and dressing, and serve.

Per serving: Calories: 105, Protein: 2 gm., Fat: 8 gm., Carbohydrates: 6 gm.

Serves 12-15
Preparation time: 20 minutes
Marinating time: 1 hour

1 small head cabbage, cut in shreds
2 medium carrots, peeled and sliced
2 zucchini or yellow crookneck squash, sliced
1 medium head of broccoli, cut into florettes
1 red pimento, chopped
1 red medium onion, finely chopped
1 medium cucumber, peeled and cubed
1 cup alfalfa sprouts
dressing:
½ cup olive oil
1 teaspoon toasted sesame oil
4 tablespoons soy sauce
juice of 1 lime
1 teaspoon finely ground sea salt
freshly ground pepper to taste

Apple-Beet Salad

Ensalada de Betabel con Manzana

Serves 8-10
Preparation time: 15 minutes
Cooking time: 20 minutes

6 medium beets, boiled until
    tender, peeled, and cut in cubes
2 medium apples, cut in cubes
    (peeled or not, as desired)
2 medium stalks celery, chopped
4 ounces ricotta cheese
¼ cup fresh lime juice
3 tablespoons light sesame oil
1 teaspoon salt, or to taste

This sweet salad is a beautiful color and is very nutritious and high in fiber.

Combine all the ingredients, chill ½ hour, and serve.

Per serving: Calories: 93, Protein: 2 gm., Fat: 6 gm., Carbohydrates: 8 gm.

Cabbage-Carrot-Pineapple Salad

Ensalada de Col, Zanahoria, y Piña

Serves 6
Preparation time: 15 minutes

2 cups cabbage, finely shredded
½ pound carrots, peeled and
    shredded
1 cup fresh or canned pineapple,
    finely chopped
½ cup golden raisins

Children like this sweet recipe. It is quick and easy to make and is very nutritious, high in fiber, and non-fat.

Combine all the ingredients and serve.

Per serving: Calories: 70, Protein: 1 gm., Fat: 0 gm., Carbohydrates: 16 gm.

Main Dishes

Platillos Principales

Swiss Enchiladas

Enchiladas Suizas

Serves 8
Preparation time: 20 minutes

These are called Swiss Enchiladas because of the yogurt and cheese. Immigrants from Switzerland, Germany, Italy, China, Lebanon, France, as well as Spain have contributed to Mexico's diverse cuisine. All of these influences are transformed in the Mexican kitchen. These enchiladas can also be filled with Tofu or Textured Vegetable Protein Mole Enchilada Filling found on page 80.

16 tortillas
3 cups Green Chile Sauce
 (page 144), heated
2 cups Jack cheese, grated
1 cup natural yogurt
½ cup green onions, chopped

Preheat the oven to 350°F. Lightly grease a rectangular, ovenproof pan. Heat a skillet and warm the tortillas one by one on both sides before dipping in the hot Green Chile Sauce. Place each tortilla on a plate, place some cheese in a line across the middle, and roll into a cylinder. Arrange in the pan and heat in the oven for 15 minutes, or until the cheese melts. Serve with the remaining hot Green Chile Sauce, yogurt, and green onions. Accompany with Mexican rice, refried beans, and a green salad.

Per serving: Calories: 318, Protein: 15 gm., Fat: 11 gm., Carbohydrates: 37 gm.

Papadzules from the Yucatan Peninsula

Papadzules de Yucatan

This dish is a specialty prepared by Mayan in the Yucatecan. Papadzules means "food for the gods."

Serves 8
Preparation time: 30 minutes
Cooking time: 10 minutes

1 pound shelled squash seeds or
   sunflower seeds
½ pound tomatoes
1 teaspoon sea salt
2 habanero chiles
2 sprigs of fresh epazote, or
   2 tablespoons dried
2 quarts water
16 corn tortillas
10 hard-boiled eggs, peeled and
   chopped, or 2 cups Textured
   Vegetable Protein Mole
   Enchilada Filling (page 80)
finely ground sea salt

Roast the squash seeds lightly in a dry skillet over medium heat. Grind them a little at a time in a blender until uniformly fine.

Boil the tomatoes, 1 teaspoon salt, the chiles, and epazote in the 2 quarts water for 5 minutes. Remove the tomatoes, peel and seed them, and save the pulp. Remove the seeds from the chiles. Blend the tomatoes and the chiles with ¼ cup of the water in which they were boiled. Correct the salt and set aside.

Stir the ground squash seeds into the water in which the tomatoes were cooked. It should make a thick sauce. Adjust the salt. Heat in a double boiler. Do not cook over direct heat. Working quickly, warm the tortillas one at a time on a comal or dry skillet. Dip in the seed sauce, place on a work plate, put a little of the egg in the middle, and roll into a tube. Arrange the filled tortillas in an ovenproof dish until ready to serve. Warm for 15 minutes in a 375°F oven. Place two spoonfuls of the warm seed sauce on each plate, then place a well-warmed filled tortilla on top of the sauce. Spoon another bit of the seed sauce on top, decorate with a large spoonful of the tomato sauce, and serve.

Per serving: Calories: 495, Protein: 21 gm., Fat: 34 gm., Carbohydrates: 25 gm.

Textured Vegetable Protein Mole Enchiladas

Serves 6
Preparation time: 3 minutes
Cooking time: 15 minutes

Thanks to Dorothy Bates who gave me the textured vegetable protein to experiment with. This recipe was a hit with our guests who said they would be willing subjects for testing more textured vegetable protein recipes in the future! You can find commercially prepared mole sauce in the US. and Mexico. It is sold in the Mexican food section of most supermarkets. If you use it in this recipe, thin it with warm water to the consistency of thick gravy, and heat through.

**2 cups Red Mole Sauce
  (page 149)**
⅓ cup olive oil
**6 cloves garlic, peeled and
  minced**
½ onion, finely chopped
**1½ cups textured vegetable
  protein granules, soaked for
  10 minutes in 1¼ cups boiling
  water**
½ teaspoon thyme
½ teaspoon cumin
1 teaspoon salt
12 corn tortillas

Prepare the Red Mole Sauce. While it is cooking, heat the olive oil, and sauté the garlic and onion for 5 minutes. Add the soaked textured vegetable protein, thyme, cumin, and salt, and stir well to combine over low heat.

Warm the tortillas one at a time on a hot comal or dry skillet, then dip in the Red Mole Sauce until soft. Place on a working plate, place a small amount of the seasoned textured vegetable protein in the middle, and roll into a tube. Arrange the filled tortillas in an ovenproof dish until ready to serve. Warm for 15 minutes in a 375°F oven. Place two on each plate, and cover with the sauce. Serve with Mexican Rice (page 128) and Tossed Salad from La Casa del Pan (page 64), with Hot Chipotle Sauce (page 148) on the side, and pineapple juice as a beverage.

Per serving: Calories: 537, Protein: 18 gm., Fat: 29 gm., Carbohydrates: 49 gm.

Enchiladas from Morelia

Enchiladas Placeras de Morelia

This is an adaptation of the enchiladas prepared by the street vendors in their rustic kitchens every evening around the beautiful, historic colonial plaza of the city of Morelia, capital of the state of Michoacan.

In a dry skillet or on a comal, roast the chiles, garlic, and onion over medium heat until aromatic. Combine in a blender with the hot water and salt, and blend until smooth. Set aside.

Cook the carrots and potatoes in the salted boiling water for 15 minutes. Drain the water into the chile sauce. Add the vinegar to the vegetables, and stir to flavor evenly.

Heat the oil in a small skillet, and fry the tortillas on both sides. Dip the tortillas into the chile sauce, coating each one with the sauce. Remove to a work plate. Sprinkle a line of queso fresco and green onions across the middle of each tortilla. Roll into a tube, place on a warm serving dish, and keep warm.

When all of the enchiladas have been formed, sprinkle the vegetables over the top, then the cheese, sour cream, lettuce, and jalapeños. Serve immediately, accompanied by black beans.

Per serving: Calories: 358, Protein: 15 gm., Fat: 12 gm., Carbohydrates: 45 gm.

Serves 5
Preparation time: 40 minutes

sauce:
3 ancho chiles
3 guajillo chiles
5 cloves garlic, peeled
1 small onion, coarsely chopped
1 cup hot water
½ teaspoon sea salt
vegetables:
1 cup carrots, peeled and chopped
2 cups boiling water
1 teaspoon salt
1 cup potatoes, peeled and cubed
½ cup apple cider vinegar
¼ cup sunflower oil
10 tortillas
filling:
1 cup (½ pound) queso fresco or farmer's cheese
½ cup scallions, chopped
garnish:
½ cup queso fresco or farmer's cheese
½ cup sour cream or plain yogurt
1 cup iceberg lettuce, shredded
¼ cup pickled jalapeños, cut in strips

San Cristobal Bread Casserole

Sopa de Pan San Cristobal

Serves 6-8
Preparation time: 30 minutes
Cooking time: 30 minutes

San Cristobal is a small colonial city nestled in the cool Mayan highlands of central Chiapas. Surrounded by archaeological sites and numerous traditional Mayan Indian groups, it is a haven for anthropologists, archaeologists, linguists, and sociologists, as well as painters and writers. This recipe is a tradition in San Cristobal and has a definite Spanish influence.

1 head of garlic, roasted in a dry skillet and then peeled
¼ cup water
sea salt to taste
freshly ground black pepper to taste
3 small carrots, sliced diagonally
½ cup peas
1½ quarts salted water
5 small zucchini squash, sliced diagonally
2 teaspoons allspice
1 tablespoon black pepper
⅛ teaspoon cloves
1 small cinnamon stick
1 teaspoon oregano
1 teaspoon cumin
½ teaspoon sea salt
1 tablespoon achiote
2 tablespoons olive oil
1 red onion, roasted in a dry skillet and then thinly sliced

Make a paste by smashing the garlic with the ¼ cup water, salt, and pepper.

Boil the carrots and peas in 1½ quarts salted water for 20 minutes. Add the squash and boil 5 more minutes. Remove the vegetables and add the allspice, black pepper, cloves, cinnamon stick, oregano, and cumin. Simmer for 15 more minutes, and add the achiote by first making a paste of it with a little of the stock, then gradually thinning it before adding to the broth.

In 2 tablespoons olive oil, sauté the onion, pimentos, almonds, olives, capers, tomatoes, raisins, and ¼ cup water, adding salt and pepper to taste.

Heat 2 tablespoons of the corn oil in a skillet, and fry ⅓ of the bread, turning to coat both sides with the oil. Repeat 2 times, until all the bread is fried. Drain on paper towels and spread with the garlic paste.

Sauté the plantains in the leftover oil. Preheat the oven to 350°F. Strain the broth.

In an ovenproof casserole, arrange a layer of half of the bread, cover it with half of the tomato mixture, then arrange a layer with half of the boiled vegetables. Repeat the layers, and then arrange the plantains and boiled egg slices on top. Pour 1 quart of the seasoned stock over the casserole, and bake in a 350°F oven for 30 minutes.

Per serving: Calories: 488, Protein: 11 gm., Fat: 23 gm., Carbohydrates: 59 gm.

2 red pimentos, roasted in a dry skillet, peeled, and sliced
¼ cup almonds, sliced
¼ cup sliced green olives
12 capers
4 medium tomatoes, roasted, peeled, seeded and chopped
¼ cup raisins
6 tablespoons corn oil
twenty 1-inch slices of day-old French bread
2 plantains, diagonally sliced
2 hard-boiled eggs, sliced

Stuffed Chayotes

Chayotes Rellenos

Serves 3
Preparation time: 15 minutes
Cooking time: 50 minutes

3 chayotes, boiled in salted water
  until tender (about 30 minutes)
2 teaspoons minced garlic
1 teaspoon fresh thyme, or
  ½ teaspoon dried
½ cup Monterey Jack cheese or
  cooked brown rice
½ cup cooked sweet corn
¼ cup stock (or butter)
salt and freshly ground pepper to
  taste
⅓ cup seasoned whole wheat or
  rye bread crumbs
¼ cup Parmesan cheese

Chayotes are pear-shaped, juicy vegetables that grow on a vine. There are two basic varieties: those with spines and those without. Homegrown varieties have spines; grocers carry the smooth ones. Both kinds are delicious just boiled and salted.

Preheat the oven to 375°F. Slice the chayotes in half lengthwise, and remove the seeds. Scoop out the pulp and save the shells. Mash the chayote and mix it with the garlic, thyme, cheese, corn, stock, salt, and pepper. Fill the chayote shells with the mixture, and cover with bread crumbs and Parmesan cheese. Arrange in an ovenproof dish, and bake for 20 minutes.

Per serving: Calories: 257, Protein: 11 gm., Fat: 7 gm., Carbohydrates: 36 gm.

chayotes

Chiles Rellenos

Stuffed with Textured Vegetable Protein Picadillo

Chile Rellenos de Picadillo

Poblano chiles are ideal for stuffing. Eduardo and Deborah of Madre Tierra Restaurant in San Cristobal approved enthusiastically of this original textured vegetable protein recipe. The flavors are quite exotic. This vegetarian version of one of the Yucatan's most famous recipes is light and delicious.

Serves 6
Preparation time: 30 minutes
Cooking time: 30 minutes

Roast the chiles on a comal, or in a wide, dry skillet. While they are still hot, place them in a plastic bag to sweat until cooled. Place them in a wide pan with cool water, and rub off the scorched Cut a slit in the side of each chile to remove the veins and seeds. Rinse well. If you plan to peel and seed more than a few chiles, you may want to wear gloves. Roast and peel the garlic.

To make the filling, blend the garlic, oregano, cloves, cinnamon, black pepper, salt, orange juice, and vinegar. Hydrate the textured vegetable protein granules in 1¾ cups hot water, stirring to moisten evenly. Roast, peel, seed, and chop the tomatoes. Heat the oil and sauté the onion for 5 minutes. Add the tomatoes and continue to sauté for 10 more minutes. Add the green olives and raisins, stir, and combine with the textured vegetable protein. Turn off the heat. Preheat the oven to 350°F. Stuff the chiles with the picadillo filling. Arrange in an ovenproof dish, and top with the grated cheese. Bake for 20 minutes and serve with warmed Mild or Hot Ranchero Sauce.

Per serving: Calories: 289, Protein: 15 gm., Fat: 9 gm., Carbohydrates: 34 gm.

12 poblano chiles
Picadillo Filling:
1 head of garlic
1 tablespoon oregano
⅛ teaspoon cloves
¼ teaspoon cinnamon
¼ teaspoon black pepper
½ teaspoon sea salt
2 tablespoons fresh squeezed
   orange juice
2 tablespoons apple vinegar
2 cups textured vegetable protein
   granules
4 tablespoons olive oil
1 red onion, chopped
4 tomatoes
15 green olives, chopped
20 raisins
½ cup grated Chihuahua or
   Monterey Jack cheese or
   croutons (optional)
1 cup Mild or Hot Ranchero
   Sauce (pages 146, 147), for
   topping

Chiles Rellenos in Walnut Sauce

Chiles en Nogada

Serves 6
Preparation time: 1 hour
Cooking time: 30 minutes

This recipe is famous throughout Mexico's altiplano (high plain). It was invented by the nuns of the city of Pueblo to offer at a banquet honoring Don Augustine de Iturbide on August 28, 1821. Iturbide was victorious in leading the final struggle for Mexican Independence from Spain. This dish displays the colors of the Mexican flag. It is traditionally served in central Mexico during the month of September, when Mexican Independence is celebrated. Begin this recipe a day ahead.

6 large poblano chiles, stuffed with Picadillo Filling (page 85)
Walnut Sauce:
30 fresh walnuts, shelled and peeled (very fresh walnuts are important)
1 cup milk, or enough to cover the walnuts
2 cups sour cream
½ teaspoon salt
pinch of cinnamon
garnish:
seeds of 1 pomegranate

Allow the walnuts to soak overnight in the milk. Prepare half of the recipe for Chiles Rellenos with Picadillo Stuffing (page 85), without the grated cheese or Ranchero Sauce topping. Preheat the oven to 375°F. Warm the stuffed chiles for 10 minutes in the oven. Meanwhile, blend the ingredients for the sauce. When the chiles are removed from the oven, serve immediately. Pour the cold sauce over them, and sprinkle with pomegranate seeds.

Per serving: Calories: 323, Protein: 14 gm., Fat: 22 gm., Carbohydrates: 16 gm.

Stuffed Ancho Chiles

Chiles Anchos Rellenos

Ancho chiles are dried poblano chiles. They are dark reddish brown, wrinkled like a prune, and mildly spicy.

In a 2-quart saucepan with a tight fitting lid, heat the rice, water, bay leaf, and salt until the water boils. Reduce the heat to low, cover the pot, and cook the rice for 20 minutes.

To prepare the chiles, soak them in the 2 quarts of hot water for 5 minutes to soften. Carefully remove the stems by cutting a circle around the top of each chile. Remove the seeds. Preheat the oven to 375°F. Stuff the chiles with the cheese. Line the bottom of a lightly oiled 9 x 12-inch ovenproof pan or casserole dish with the rice, and arrange the stuffed chiles on top. Cover with aluminum foil and bake for 20 minutes until the cheese has barely melted. Serve with the cream poured over the top.

Per serving: Calories: 669, Protein: 30 gm., Fat: 32 gm., Carbohydrates: 61 gm.

Serves 6
Preparation time: 20 minutes
Cooking time: 40 minutes

3 cups rice
6 cups water
1 bay leaf
½ teaspoon sea salt
12 small ancho chiles
2 quarts hot water
1 pound Chihuahua or Monterey
   Jack cheese, grated
2 cups sour cream

chiles anchos

Baked Chiles Rellenos

Chiles Rellenos Horneados

Serves 4
Preparation time: 20 minutes
Baking time: 20 minutes

**4 large poblano chiles or 8 small
ones, or two 4-ounce cans of
green chiles**
**½ pound Chihuahua, Muenster,
or Monterey Jack cheese, grated**
4 eggs, separated
¼ cup flour
½ teaspoon baking powder
½ teaspoon sea salt
sauce:
½ pound tomatoes
2 cloves garlic, peeled
½ onion
1 sprig fresh epazote or parsley
pinch of sea salt

*Here is an alternative to deep-fat frying chile
rellenos.*

Preheat the oven to 350°F. To peel the chiles,
first roast them on a hot griddle or under the broiler, turning occasionally until they are evenly blis-
tered. Place them in plastic bag to sweat for a few
minutes, then peel. Cut a slit down the side of each
chile. Remove the seeds and veins with care. If the
chiles are hot, they may burn your fingers. To remedy this you can soak them in salt water for 15
minutes and wash your hands after handling
them. You can also use plastic gloves to handle the
chiles.

Stuff the chiles with the cheese, and place in a
lightly oiled 9 x 9-inch baking dish. Beat the egg
whites until stiff but not dry. Separately, beat the
yolks slightly, adding the flour, baking powder,
and salt. Fold the yolk mixture into the beaten egg
whites until well blended. Pour this mixture over
the chiles, and bake for 20 minutes.

Meanwhile, blend the tomatoes with the garlic
and onion. Strain through a fine wire strainer into
a small pot. Cook with the epazote and salt over
low heat while the chiles bake. When the chiles are
done, remove them from the oven, and serve with
the tomato sauce on top, accompanied by refried
beans.

*Per serving: Calories: 359, Protein: 24 gm., Fat: 22 gm.,
Carbohydrates: 14 gm.*

Chiles Rellenos Stuffed With Brown Rice

Chiles Rellenos de Arroz Integral

Follow the instructions for peeling, seeding, and handling chiles as given in the recipe for Baked Chiles Rellenos (page 88). These chiles are also baked and fat-free.

Preheat the oven to 375°F. Cut a slit in the sides of the chiles for stuffing. (Do not remove the stems.) Remove the seeds and veins. Rinse well and soak for 15 minutes in salted water to lessen their fire. Combine the rice with the chipilín, onions, and salt, and fill the chilies with this mixture. Arrange the chiles in a lightly oiled, 9 x 9-inch baking dish, and bake for 20 minutes. Make a sauce by heating the refried beans with the water, mixing well over low heat while the chiles bake. To serve, spoon the bean sauce over each chile, and garnish with a spoonful of sour cream and green onions.

Per serving: Calories: 352, Protein: 12 gm., Fat: 1 gm., Carbohydrates: 72 gm.

Serves 4
Preparation time: 20 minutes
Baking time: 20 minutes

4 large poblano chiles, or
    3 small ones, peeled, seeded,
    and deveined
3 cups cooked brown rice
¼ cup chipilín, cilantro, or
    parsley, chopped
4 green onions, chopped
½ teaspoon sea salt
2 cups Refried Beans (page 123)
1 cup water
1 pint sour cream (optional)
½ cup green onions, chopped
    (optional)

Baked Chilaquiles

Chilaquiles Horneados

Serves 4-6
Preparation time: 20 minutes
Cooking time: 20 minutes

Here is a great solution for leftover tortillas that is delicious and easy to make–an all-time favorite. There are many variations. This one uses green tomatillos, a small, green variety of wild tomato which grows with a thin, leaflike husk. The husk is removed before cooking the tomatillos.

12 tortillas, cut in strips
3 tablespoons oil
4 cloves garlic, roasted and
   smashed
1 small onion, roasted and sliced
1 pound green tomatillos,
   husked, boiled for 15 minutes
   in salt water, and drained
1 cup water
sea salt to taste
¾ cup Chihuahua or Monterey
   Jack cheese, grated
1 cup plain yogurt
3 green onions, chopped

Preheat the oven to 350°F. Fry the tortilla strips in the oil until crispy. Roast the garlic and onion on a comal or dry skillet over medium heat, turning to scorch evenly. Combine the garlic, onion, tomatillos, and water in a blender Add salt to taste. In an ovenproof dish, layer the tortilla strips, then the cheese, and then the sauce. Repeat the layers. Bake for 20 minutes.

Remove from the oven and garnish with the yogurt and green onions.

Per serving: Calories: 309, Protein: 13 gm., Fat: 10 gm., Carbohydrates: 39 gm.

Aztec Pie

Pay Azteca

Carmen Bastida cooks for Ingrid Primus, a beautiful Swedish immigrant whose gallery, "L'Arlequin," on the colonial street of Francisco Sosa in Coyoacan, is a very rewarding place to shop in Mexico City. When I asked Ingrid if she'd like to contribute this very popular recipe to the book, she referred me to Carmen, who was delighted to share it.

Serves 8-10
Preparation time: 30 minutes
Cooking time: 30 minutes

Sauté the tortillas lightly in the ¼ cup of oil, and drain on paper towels. Prepare the sauce by sautéing the onion in the 1½ tablespoons of oil 5 for minutes, then add the tomatoes. Continue to sauté until the tomato becomes saucy. Add the tomato purée, epazote, water, and salt, and simmer for 10 minutes. Add the corn and strips of poblano chile. Preheat the oven to 350°F. In a large ovenproof casserole, arrange ⅓ of the tortillas, and cover with ⅓ of the sauce, ⅓ of the sour cream, and ⅓ of the cheese. Repeat this layer twice, ending with the cheese on top. Bake for 30 minutes. Serve with tossed green salad.

Per serving: Calories: 487, Protein: 16 gm., Fat: 24 gm., Carbohydrates: 47 gm.

20 corn tortillas
¼ cup sunflower oil for frying
kernels from 3 ears of boiled corn, cut from the cob
2 pounds poblano chiles, roasted, peeled, seeded, and cut in strips
2 cups sour cream
½ pound Manchego cheese, Monterrey Jack, or cheddar, grated
sauce:
¼ onion, sliced
1½ tablespoons oil
2 tomatoes, peeled, seeded, and chopped
3 cups tomato purée
1 generous sprig fresh epazote
½ cup water
sea salt to taste

Mexican Quiche from La Casa del Pan

Quiche Mexicana de la Casa Del Pan

Serves 8 to 10
Preparation time: 20 minutes
Cooking time: 40 minutes
Chilling time (for dough): 2 hours

dough:
1 cup butter (at room temperature)
1 teaspoon fine sea salt
4 cups whole wheat pastry flour
1⅓ cups water

filling:
½ cup green onions, chopped
2 tablespoons sunflower oil
½ pound poblano chiles, roasted, peeled, and cut in strips
1⅓ cup cooked corn kernels
½ pound squash blossoms or spinach, chopped
1 quart milk
1½ cups Gruyere cheese, grated
6 eggs

The combination of poblano chile, corn, and squash blossoms is a Mexican dream. It makes a delicious and original quiche, which may be served hot or cold.

Prepare the dough by combining the butter, salt, and flour, using your hands to mix. When the mixture is uniform, add the water, and stir with a spiral movement. Cover with a damp cloth, and refrigerate for 2 to 36 hours.

Prepare the filling by sautéing the green onions in the oil for 3 minutes. Add the strips of chile, corn, and squash blossoms. Sauté for 5 minutes and remove from heat. Heat the milk and beat the eggs. Separate one of the egg whites and reserve for brushing the dough. Add the milk to the eggs gradually, to avoid cooking the eggs.

Preheat the oven to 375°F. Roll out the dough on a floured board, to a thickness of ⅜ inch. Place in a pie pan, and prick with a fork. Brush with the reserved egg white. Pour the filling into the pie pan, and cover it with the milk and egg mixture. Bake for 40 minutes or until brown.

Per serving: Calories: 610, Protein: 22 gm., Fat: 35 gm., Carbohydrates: 48 gm.

Oatmeal Patties

Tortitas de Avena

Flora Sanchez from Guadalajara taught me this outstanding recipe. The tortitas also make fine burgers, served on a sourdough roll with all of the trimmings. Use raw rolled oats for this recipe, not instant oatmeal.

Soak the sesame seeds for the sauce overnight in ¼ cup water, drain, and rinse.

Mix the oats with the milk, and allow to sit for 2 hours, so the milk will be absorbed. Knead with your fingers before adding the rest of the ingredients, then mix everything together well, and form patties 3 inches in diameter, ½ inch thick. Heat 1 tablespoon oil in a wide, nonstick skillet, and fry the patties over medium heat, about 3 minutes on each side or until browned evenly. Serve with Sesame-Avocado Sauce.

To make the sauce, blend the sesame seeds, parsley, onion, soy sauce, avocados, garlic, and water, together in a blender until smooth, and serve alongside the tortitas

Per serving: Calories: 269, Protein: 12 gm., Fat: 10 gm., Carbohydrates: 30 gm.

Serves 6-8
Preparation and Cooking time:
1 hour

½ pound rolled oats
1 cup milk
¼ pound mozzarella cheese, grated
½ medium onion, chopped
1 medium carrot, grated
1 medium zucchini squash, grated
¼ cup fresh parsley, chopped
1 tablespoon fresh marjoram, or 1 teaspoon dried
1 tablespoon fresh rosemary, or 1 teaspoon dried
2 teaspoons soy sauce
sea salt to taste
freshly ground pepper to taste
vegetable oil for frying
Sesame-Avocado Sauce:
2 tablespoons sesame seeds
¼ cup fresh parsley, chopped
3 tablespoons medium onion, chopped
2 teaspoons soy sauce
1 large avocado
1 clove garlic, scorched in a dry skillet and peeled
½ cup water

Mole Crepes

Crepas de Mole

Serves 8
Preparation time: 30 minutes
Cooking time: 30 minutes

crepes:
1 egg
2 cups milk
1 cup flour
1 tablespoon melted butter
   butter for frying the crepes
filling:
3 tablespoons sesame oil
¼ cup onions, chopped
1 cup zucchini or yellow
   crookneck squash, chopped
1 cup mushrooms, thinly sliced
½ teaspoon marjoram
sea salt to taste
Mole Sauce:
5 guajillo chiles
3 ancho chiles , deseeded and
   deveined
1 small, whole onion
5 whole cloves garlic
½ teaspoon thyme
½ teaspoon marjoram
¼ cup sesame seeds
4 Italian tomatoes, roasted and
   peeled
⅓ cup sesame or sunflower oil
3 plantains, sliced

The same sauce that is used for enchiladas can be used for crepes, which, if not strictly traditional, are popular in Mexico's finest restaurants.

To prepare the crepes, beat the egg with the milk, flour, and melted butter. Heat a 6-inch non-stick skillet with rounded sides over medium heat. Melt ½ teaspoon of butter, and spread it around the bottom of the skillet. Add 2 tablespoons of the crepe mixture to the pan, and rotate the skillet until the batter covers the bottom. When the edges of the crepe begin to dry out, turn the crepe over (either with a spatula or by flipping the crepe), and cook until it barely begins to brown. Remove it to a plate, and repeat the process until all the batter has been used (about 16-20 crepes).

To prepare the filling, heat the oil in a large skillet, and sauté the onions for 3 minutes. Add the squash and mushrooms, and sauté for 5 more minutes. Add the marjoram and salt, and continue to cook over medium heat, stirring occasionally, for 10 minutes. Reserve.

To prepare the sauce, roast the chiles on a hot comal or in a dry frying pan for 5 minutes, turning occasionally. Immerse in enough hot water to cover for 15 minutes, then seed, devein, and chop. Meanwhile, roast the onion, garlic, thyme, marjoram, sesame seeds, and tomatoes on the comal or in the same skillet as the chiles. Set aside. Heat the oil in the skillet, and sauté the plantains until they begin to brown; remove to a plate. Sauté the sliced *bolillos*. Blend all the sauce ingredients (including the chocolate, water, and salt), then simmer the purée in the skillet for 10 minutes on low heat, stirring to prevent sticking. Preheat the oven to 350°F.

To assemble the crepes, place 1 tablespoon of the filling in a line across the middle of a crepe. Roll the crepe into a tube, with the filling inside. Place inside a lightly buttered, rectangular oven-proof casserole or baking pan. Repeat until all the crepes have been filled and placed in the pan. Cover with the sauce, then with the cheese. Cover with the casserole lid or aluminum foil, and bake until bubbly, about 25 minutes. Sprinkle with sesame seeds. This recipe can be prepared ahead of time, leaving the baking until the guests begin to eat the first course.

Per serving: Calories: 626, Protein: 16 gm., Fat: 37 gm., Carbohydrates: 55 gm.

2 bolillos (crusty rolls, similar to baguettes), sliced
½ cup (4 ounces) bitter baking chocolate
½ cup water
1 teaspoon salt, or to taste
garnish:
1 cup Chihuahua, Manchego or other white cheese, grated
¼ cup toasted sesame seeds

Chayote Root Veracruz Style

Cueza a la Veracruzana

Serves 10-12
Preparation time: 20 minutes
Cooking time: 1 hour

3 pounds cueza, peeled and cut
   in 1-inch slices
8 cloves garlic, chopped
1 cup onion, finely chopped
2 tablespoons olive oil
4 pounds tomatoes, peeled,
   seeded, and chopped
2 pimentos, cut in strips
1 tablespoon sea salt
1 teaspoon black pepper, freshly
   ground
4 bay leaves
1 teaspoon oregano
4 tablespoons butter
½ cup stuffed green olives,
   sliced
½ cup capers
12 guero chiles, whole (fresh or
   canned)

This delectable recipe for the root of the chayote, "cueza," is an adaptation of a traditional Veracruz recipe for fish. If you can't find or grow the cueza, you may substitute potatoes.

Boil the cueza in salted water for 20 minutes, drain, and reserve. While the cueza is cooking, sauté the garlic and onion in the oil for 3 minutes. Add the tomatoes and bring to a boil. Add the pimentos and cook, stirring, for 2 more minutes. Add the salt, black pepper, bay leaves, and oregano, cover, and cook over low heat for 10 minutes. Turn off the heat. Preheat the oven to 375°F. Sauté the cueza in the butter until golden brown, turning to brown both sides. Arrange the browned cueza in an ovenproof baking dish, cover with the tomato mixture, and sprinkle the olives, capers, and guero chiles on top. Cover with banana leaves (or aluminum foil), and bake for 25 minutes or until bubbly. Serve with green salad or sautéed spinach.

Per serving: Calories: 217, Protein: 3 gm., Fat: 7 gm., Carbohydrates: 35 gm.

Romeritos

Romeritos are feathery-leafed greens, similar in appearance to rosemary, but mild in flavor. They are almost impossible to find outside of Mexico, and even there they are difficult to find. This dish is traditional in central and northern Mexico at Christmas, where it is served with tortitas de camarón (shrimp cakes). In this recipe, potato cakes are substituted. To substitute the romeritos would be impossible, so this recipe is limited to their availability. They may be ordered ahead of time from especially accommodating Mexican specialty shops, if there is sufficient demand for them in your area; otherwise, save this recipe for preparing when you're in Mexico around Christmas or New Year's Eve.

Wash the romeritos, remove the stems, and cook for 3 minutes in the boiling water. Remove from the water and reserve. Add the nopales, onion, and salt, and boil for 25 minutes. Strain and rinse several times in cold water. Heat the oil in a 4-quart saucepan, and sauté the nopales for 10 minutes. Add the Mole Sauce, stir, heat through, add the romeritos, and cook for 5 minutes.

To make the potato cakes, boil the potatoes in enough water to cover until tender (about 20 minutes). Mash (with skins) with a fork, add the salt, flour, milk, and eggs, and form into flattened rounds about 2 inches in diameter. Heat the oil in a skillet, and fry the potato cakes on both sides until they begin to brown. Remove to a paper towel, and keep in a warm (150°F) oven until ready to serve with the Romerito-Nopal sauce poured over.

Per serving: Calories: 550, Protein: 11 gm., Fat: 35 gm., Carbohydrates: 43 gm.

Serves 8
Preparation time: 45 minutes
Cooking time: 1 hour

Romerito-Nopal Sauce:
2 pounds romeritos
1 quart boiling water
5 nopales, with spines removed, and cut into 2-inch strips
1 large onion, sliced
2 tablespoons sea salt (for boiling the nopales)
¼ cup sesame oil, or sunflower oil
1 quart Red Mole Sauce (page 149)
salt to taste
Potato Cakes:
1 pound potatoes, unpeeled and quartered
1 teaspoon sea salt
¼ cup flour
½ cup milk
2 eggs, slightly beaten
¼ cup sesame oil for frying

Huitlacoche Crepes with Poblano Chiles Sauce

Crepas de Huitlacoche Con Salsa de Chiles Poblanos

Serves 8
Preparation time: 45 minutes
Cooking time: 25 minutes

Huitlacoche is a dark gray fungus that grows on corn in the field. American farmers call it "smut" and throw it away as an unwanted plague. Mexican farmers prize it, since it is considered a delicacy and fetches a high price at the market. Mexican cooks prepare it as a filling for tacos. When I can't get huitlacoche, I substitute a combination of Swiss chard and mushrooms, with delicious results.

crepes:
1 egg
2 cups milk
1 cup flour
1 tablespoon melted butter
additional butter for frying the crepes
filling:
3 tablespoons cold-pressed sesame oil
⅓ cup scallions, chopped
½ cup fresh corn kernels
1 sprig fresh epazote, chopped (about 1 tablespoon)
½ pound fresh huitlacoche, or two 4 ounce cans
sea salt to taste

To prepare the crepes, beat the egg with the milk, flour, and melted butter. Heat a 6-inch nonstick, rounded skillet over medium heat. Melt ½ teaspoon of butter, and spread it around the bottom of the skillet. Add 2 tablespoons of the crepe mixture to the pan, and rotate the skillet until the batter covers the bottom. When the edges of the crepe begin to dry out, turn the crepe over (either with a spatula or by flipping the crepe), and cook until it barely begins to brown. Remove it to a plate, and repeat the process until all the batter has been used (about 16-20 crepes).

To prepare the filling, heat the oil in a large skillet, and sauté the scallions for 3 minutes. Add the corn and epazote, and sauté for 5 more minutes. Add the huitlacoche, and continue to cook, over medium heat, stirring occasionally, for 10 minutes. Season with salt and set aside.

To prepare the sauce, blend the chiles with ⅓ cup milk. In a medium skillet over low heat, melt the butter and add the flour, stirring constantly. Gradually stir in the sour cream. Then gradually add 1 cup milk, continuing to stir. Add the salt and cook, stirring until the sauce thickens. Add the blended chiles, cook over low heat for 5 minutes, and remove from the heat. Preheat the oven to 350°F.

To assemble the crepes, place 1 tablespoon of the filling in a line across the middle of a crepe. Roll the crepe into a tube with the filling inside. Place inside a lightly buttered, rectangular, oven-proof casserole or baking pan. Repeat until all the crepes have been filled and placed in the pan. Cover with the sauce and then with the cheese. Cover with a casserole lid or aluminum foil, and bake at 350°F until bubbly, about 25 minutes. This recipe can be prepared ahead of time, leaving the baking until the guests begin to eat the first course.

Per serving: Calories: 330, Protein: 11 gm., Fat: 22 gm., Carbohydrates: 21 gm.

sauce:
2 poblano chiles, seeded and deveined
⅓ cup milk
¼ cup butter
2 tablespoons flour
1 cup sour cream
1 cup milk
1 teaspoon salt, or to taste
topping:
1 cup Chihuahua or other white cheese, grated

Lentil-Nut Loaf

Pastel de Lenteja con Nuez

Serves
Preparation time: 25 minutes
Cooking time: 1 hour 15 minutes

1 tablespoon vegetable oil
1 tablespoon onion, finely
   chopped
3 celery ribs, chopped
2 chipotle chiles, chopped
1 pound lentils, well washed
1½ quarts water
¼ cup parsley, chopped
½ pound pecans, chopped
½ cup bread crumbs
1 tablespoon soy sauce
½ teaspoon salt, or to taste
tomato sauce:
2 tablespoons vegetable oil
1 tablespoon onion, finely
   chopped
2 pounds tomatoes
   (about 5½ cups), chopped
1 cup water or vegetable stock
1 bay leaf
½ teaspoon sea salt
freshly ground black pepper

This is a high-protein dish, very flavorful, with a subtle hint of smoke from the chipotle chiles.

Heat the oil in the bottom of a pressure cooker, and sauté the onion, celery, and chiles for 5 minutes. Add the lentils and cover them with the 1½ quarts water. Close the pressure cooker and cook over medium heat for 30 minutes, or until the lentils are soft and dry. If you don't have a pressure cooker, boil the lentils in the water, covered, over low heat until tender, about 1½ hours. Add the parsley, pecans, bread crumbs, soy sauce, and salt, and mix well, forming a heavy dough.

Preheat the oven to 350°F. Line a 5 x 9-inch bread pan with aluminum foil, and grease it with butter. Fill the pan with the lentil mixture, and cover with a piece of aluminum foil to seal in the moisture. Bake for 45 minutes.

While the lentil loaf is in the oven, prepare the tomato sauce by heating the oil in a 2-quart saucepan, and sautéing the onion for 5 minutes. Add the tomatoes and cook for 15 minutes over low heat, stirring occasionally. Add the water, bay leaf, salt, and black pepper, cover and allow to cook over low heat for 45 minutes, stirring occasionally.

When the loaf is done baking, remove from the oven and allow to stand 5 minutes before removing from the pan. Decorate with pecan halves, and serve sliced, covered with hot tomato sauce.

Per serving: Calories: 489, Protein: 14 gm., Fat: 25 gm., Carbohydrates: 48 gm.

Spanish Potato Tortilla

Tortilla de Patata

Many of Mexico's recipes originated in Spain, where a considerable amount of oil is used. This recipe was taught to me by a young Spaniard named Juan, who worked at La Casa del Pan. I've reduced the oil by half, and most of this is drained off after frying the potatoes.

Serves 6
Preparation time: 10 minutes
Cooking time: 30 minutes

Fry the potatoes in the oil until cooked, then add the onions, and fry another 5 minutes. Remove from the pan and drain off the excess oil. Combine the potatoes and onions with the beaten egg, and return to the skillet. Cook over medium heat until the bottom begins to brown. Turn onto a large plate. Return to the skillet, this time with the browned side on top, and cook for another 3 minutes or until the second side begins to brown. Remove to a serving platter, and serve with pickled chiles and salad.

Per serving: Calories: 393, Protein: 12 gm., Fat: 16 gm., Carbohydrates: 49 gm.

3 pounds potatoes, peeled and chopped
1 cup vegetable oil
½ pound onions, sliced
8 eggs, beaten
1 teaspoon finely ground sea salt, or to taste
freshly ground black pepper

Stuffed Squash
Calabacin Rellenos

Serves 6
Preparation time: 15 minutes
Baking time: 15 minutes

1 cup boiling water
1 cup textured vegetable protein granules
6 large zucchini (about 8 inches long)
¼ cup scallions, chopped
1 jalapeño chile, minced
¼ cup red pimento, chopped
1 teaspoon sea salt
¼ cup grated cheese for garnish (optional)

Use large zucchini for this recipe, which can be prepared ahead of time, refrigerated, and then baked one hour before serving.

Preheat the oven to 350°F. Pour the 1 cup boiling water over the textured vegetable protein, stir, and let stand 5-10 minutes. Meanwhile, boil the zucchini whole for 10 minutes. Cut in half lengthwise, and scoop out the insides. Mash them together with the textured vegetable protein, scallions, jalapeño, pimento, and sea salt. Fill the zucchini shells with this mixture, and cover with grated cheese. Bake for 15 minutes or until bubbly.

If you refrigerate this before baking, be sure to bake for 1 hour to allow the squash to thoroughly heat through.

Per serving: Calories: 64, Protein: 8 gm., Fat: 0 gm., Carbohydrates: 8 gm.

jalapeños

Zucchini Pudding

Budin de Calabacin

This simple recipe is very rewarding. It melts in your mouth and is full of flavor.

Serves 6
Preparation time: 15 minutes
Cooking time: 40 minutes

Cook the zucchini in the boiling water until tender, about 20 minutes. Preheat the oven to 350°F. Smash the zucchini with a potato masher in a wide bowl. Mix them with the cheese (saving some for the top), the egg, bread crumbs, and butter. Season with the nutmeg, salt, and black pepper. Place in a buttered 9 x 12-inch baking dish, cover with the remaining cheese, and bake for 15-20 minutes until the cheese begins to brown. Serve with salad.

Per serving: Calories: 196, Protein: 7 gm., Fat: 15 gm., Carbohydrates: 8 gm.

1 pound zucchini squash, chopped
2 cups boiling water
¼ pound white cheddar cheese, grated
1 egg, beaten
1 cup whole wheat bread crumbs
¼ cup soft butter
grating of nutmeg
salt to taste
black pepper to taste

Tamales

I first experienced the fun of making tamales in the home of my friend, Carmen Downing, a full-blooded Zapotec woman from Oaxaca. Everyone joins in—beating the dough and kneading it, preparing the sauce and fillings, forming each tamal, and then putting them on to steam. Making them is as much a fiesta as eating them. There are endless possibilities for fillings, and every region in Mexico has its specialties.

There are many kinds of tamales, savory and sweet, throughout Mexico. It is speculated by some archaeologists that pre-Hispanic Mexicans thrived on tamales, before they invented tortillas, which depend on a comal to produce.

The tamale is an ideal type of food: it is delicious, nutritious, hygienic, and ecological (it comes in its own biodegradable wrapping). To make tamales, you must obtain either dehydrated masa flour (also called instant masa or masa harina) which is available in most supermarkets, or fresh tortilla masa, available at tortilla factories. If there is a corn-grinding mill near you, or if you have a hand mill, you may wish to boil and grind your own corn. Instructions for grinding and cooking the corn are given so you may make your tamales from scratch. You must also obtain dried corn husks or banana leaves to wrap the tamales in while they are steamed. (This wrapping is also perfect for storing and transporting the tamales, and the tamale is not a tamale without it.) The dried corn husks can be purchased at many supermarkets in the specialty foods section, or at Mexican markets or friendly restaurants. (If they won't sell them, they may be able to tell you where you can find them.) Green husks may also be used, or they can be dried for future use. Dry them in a sunny place; store them in a cool, dry place. The banana leaves are more difficult to find, but they are sometimes available in specialty markets in large urban areas.

Recipes for 28 to 30 tamales may sound large, but you won't regret it. They freeze very well. Tamales can be reheated in a steamer and served in minutes. If you can organize your friends and family to join you in making the tamales, you'll have lots of fun!

Making Tamales

The basic procedure for making tamales is as follows:

1. Soak the husks (if you use dried ones) in warm water until soft. Separate them to facilitate softening. Clean them of any dirt. Use 1 large husk or two small ones per tamale, and make 2 or 3 tamales per person.

2. Prepare the filling or fillings you will be using.

3. Prepare the masa dough.

4. Spread a husk with the masa dough, as shown, and place a couple of tablespoons of filling in the middle.

5. Fold the husk around the dough to form a packet that seals in the filling.

6. Arrange the tamales in a steamer in a circular pattern, leaving a space in the middle to pour in the hot water. Steam for 1 hour. If you don't have a steamer, you can make one. Place a rack or clean jar lids in the bottom of a large pot. Cover this with clean corn husks spread flat, and layer the tamales on top.

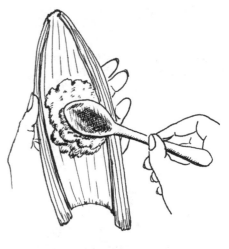

Tamale Dough from Dry Corn

Makes 4½ pounds (enough for 30
large tamales)
Serves 15
Preparation time: 20 minutes
Cooking time: 1½ hours

2½ tablespoons ground lime
2½ pounds whole dried corn
3 quarts water

Clean the corn of rocks or debris, rinse, and place in an unglazed, ceramic or enamel pot. Dissolve the lime in 1 cup water, working it with your ringers to remove any lumps. Pour into the pot with the corn. Leave the coarse lime residue at the bottom of the cup. Cook over high heat until the corn is soft, about 1½ hours, adding water as necessary. Rinse the corn thoroughly, using several changes of water. Drain and grind.

Per serving: Calories: 32, Protein: 1 gm., Fat: 0 gm., Carbohydrates: 7 gm.

Tamale Dough from Masa Flour

Makes 30 large tamales
Serves 15
Preparation time: 10 minutes
Cooking time: 1 hour

8 cups dehydrated masa flour
(masa harina)
5½ cups room temperature water
4 teaspoons sea salt
2½ cups corn oil

Combine the masa flour, water, salt, and oil, and knead until the dough is smooth (about 10 minutes).

Per serving: Calories: 275, Protein: 2 gm., Fat: 18 gm., Carbohydrates: 24 gm.

Tamale Dough from Fresh Masa

Makes 30 large tamales
Serves 15
Preparation time: 10 minutes
Cooking time: 1 hour

4½ pounds fresh corn masa
(should be moist)
2 cups corn oil or butter (at room
temperature)
2 tablespoons fine sea salt

This recipe may be made with butter or oil with good results. Personally, I like both. The Mayan women in Chiapas use only water for their delicious whole-bean tamales wrapped in banana leaves.

If using butter, beat until fluffy, then gradually add the masa and add the salt while still beating. If using oil, simply combine all the ingredients, then beat until smooth and soft.

Per serving: Calories: 184, Protein: 1 gm., Fat: 13 gm., Carbohydrates: 12 gm.

Chile-Black Bean Tamales

Chile con Frijol Negro Tamales

Makes enough filling for 25-30 tamales

Preparation time: 45 minutes

Cooking time: 1 hour

4 to 6 cloves garlic, peeled and minced

1 small onion, finely chopped

1 tablespoon olive oil

1 medium pimento, finely chopped

2 medium poblano chiles, roasted, peeled, and chopped

6 Italian tomatoes, peeled and chopped

sea salt to taste

2 cups Refried Beans (page 123)

¼ pound farmer's cheese or queso panela, cut into ½-inch cubes (optional)

Sauté the garlic and onion in the oil over medium heat for 5 minutes. Add the pimento, the poblano chiles, and tomatoes, and continue to cook, stirring constantly. Season to taste with sea salt, and remove from the heat. Place the beans and cheese in separate bowls.

Using a softened corn husk (see instructions for Tamales, page 108), spread about ¼ cup of tamale dough up and out from the base of the husk, using the back of a soup spoon. Spoon about 1 tablespoon of the tomato-chile mixture into the center of the masa, then place 2 chunks of cheese and a spoonful of beans on top. Cover the filling by folding over the sides of the dough-spread husk, then fold over the pointed ends of the husk, completely encasing the filling. You may tie the ends closed with strips of softened husk, if desired.

Arrange the tamales in a large steamer with 2-3 inches of water in the bottom. Cover and steam for 1 hour, occasionally adding hot water to replace what boils off. The steaming may be done just before serving, or the tamales may be steamed ahead of time, cooled, stored in the refrigerator, and reheated in the steamer for 10 minutes before serving.

Per tamale: Calories: 321, Protein: 4 gm., Fat: 19 gm., Carbohydrates: 30 gm.

Mumo and Black Bean Tamales

Mumo y Frijol Negro Tamales

Makes 25 to 30 tamales
Preparation time: 45 minutes
Cooking time: 1 hour

Mumo, as the Mayan Indians call it, or hierba santa as it is known in Oaxaca, is an aromatic broad leaf that grows on a tall bush in mild climates. The Indians claim it is a stomach remedy. It may be impossible to find outside of Mexico. As a substitute in this recipe, broad-leafed spinach or Swiss chard are acceptable, although they lack the pungent aroma and flavor of mumo.

4½ pounds tamale dough (see Tamale Dough recipes page 106)
1½ cups Refried Beans (page 123)
15 mumo leaves, cut in half, or 20 spinach or Swiss chard leaves, washed and dried
30 corn husks, softened in warm water for 1 hour

Divide the dough into 30 balls of equal size (about ½ cup each one). Spread each one onto a mumo leaf, and spread the beans over the top. Fold the edges into the middle, roll into a package, and place this package in the middle of a corn husk. Fold the sides of the husk over the masa-bean-leaf package, then tie the ends of the husks with strips of husk. Layer the tamales in a steamer with 5 inches of water in the bottom, cover with a clean cloth, and then with a tight-fitting lid, and steam for 1 hour.

Per tamale: Calories: 303, Protein: 4 gm., Fat: 18 gm., Carbohydrates: 28 gm.

Chipilín with Cheese Tamales

Chipilín con Queso Tamales

Chipilín is an herb native to Chiapas, mild in flavor, with small, round leaves. Chopped spinach makes a fine substitute. These tamales are traditionally wrapped in banana leaves. Ask at a good Mexican restaurant where you can find them or substitute corn husks.

Makes 20 tamales
Preparation time: 45 minutes
Cooking time: 1 hour

Knead the chipilín (or spinach) into the tamale dough. Heat the banana leaves slightly over a medium flame on the stove to soften. Wipe both sides of each leaf with a damp cloth to clean, and set aside. Shape ½ cup of dough into a flattened, oblong ball. Make an indentation in the middle large enough to hold 1 tablespoon of the cheese plus 1 teaspoon of the Mild or Hot Ranchero Sauce. Fold over the edges of the dough to cover, and seal in the cheese and sauce. Place the tamale lengthwise in the middle of a banana leaf rectangle. Fold the sides over the tamale, then the top and bottom edges. Layer the tamales into a steamer which has 5 inches of water in the bottom, cover with a clean cloth and a tight-fitting lid, and steam over medium heat for 1 hour.

Per tamale: Calories: 323, Protein: 6 gm., Fat: 21 gm., Carbohydrates: 25 gm.

3 cups chipilín or spinach, washed, stems removed, and chopped
10 cups Tamale Dough (page 106) for 20 tamales
8 medium banana leaf sections, each cut into 3 rectangles of equal size (or use 20 large corn husks, softened in warm water)
½ pound Oaxaca string cheese, Chihuahua cheese, or other white cheese, grated
1 cup Mild or Hot Ranchero Sauce (pages 146, 147)

Vegetable Tamales

Tamles de Verdura

Makes 20 tamales
Preparation time: 20 minutes
Cooking time: 1 hour

**7 cups Tamale Dough for 20
tamales (page 104)**
1 tablespoon corn oil
½ medium onion, chopped
1 cup cooked peas
**½ cup carrots, chopped and
cooked**
¼ cup green olives, chopped
**1 cup tomatoes, peeled, seeded,
and chopped**
**1 serrano chile, seeded and
chopped (optional)**
½ teaspoon dried marjoram
½ teaspoon salt, or to taste

Heat the oil in skillet, and sauté the onion until it is translucent. Add the rest of the ingredients, and cook over medium heat for 15 minutes, stirring occasionally.

*Per tamale: Calories: 293, Protein: 3 gm., Fat: 18 gm.,
Carbohydrates: 26 gm.*

"Tinga Poblana" Soy Sausage Tacos

Tinga Poblana

This soy-based dish makes a delicious filling for tacos or chiles rellenos.

Serves 6-8
Preparation and cooking time:
1 hour

Pour the boiling water over the textured vegetable protein granules, stir, and let stand for 15 minutes. Combine the achiote with the textured vegetable protein. Heat the oil in a 2-quart saucepan, and sauté the garlic and onions for 5 minutes, then add the sausage and sauté for 5 more minutes. Add the tomatoes, then the blended and whole chipotle chiles. Cover and cook over low heat for 45 minutes. Add salt to taste, cook 5 more minutes, and serve with warm tortillas and a tossed green salad.

Per serving: Calories: 409, Protein: 21 gm., Fat: 21 gm., Carbohydrates: 32 gm.

1¾ cups boiling water
2 cups textured vegetable protein granules
20 grams achiote, dissolved in ½ cup hot water
½ cup vegetable oil
6 cloves garlic, peeled and mashed
3 medium onions, chopped
½ pound spicy soy sausage
4 pounds tomatoes, roasted, peeled, and mashed
6 chipotle chiles, softened in hot water and blended
6 whole chipotle chiles
salt to taste

Yellow Mole

Mole Amarillo

Serves 10-12
Preparation time: 1 hour
Cooking time: 2 hours

Mole means sauce. This recipe is traditional in Oaxaca, where you can ask for it by simply saying, "amarillo" in the market's restaurant stalls. In Oaxaca, it is traditional to use chicken, but in this recipe, the succulent chayote makes a delicious substitute. The distinctive, aromatic flavor of yellow mole comes from the hierba santa leaf. That means holy herb, a name that honors its medicinal properties as a cure for stomach ache, an antidote for poison, and a stimulant for fevers. The root is the part used for medicine. In Chiapas, the herb is known by the Mayan Indians as mumo or mumun, where it is used as a wrapping to steam Bean Tamales (page 104). Cilantro makes an acceptable substitute in this recipe. The masa may be made with packaged dried masa (sometimes known as minsa or masa harina) and water. Follow the directions on the package.

¼ pound yellow guajillo chiles, seeded and deveined
¼ cup vegetable oil
2 medium onions, sliced in half
4 cloves garlic
1 pound tomatillos, husked
3 Italian tomatoes
5 whole cloves
1 cinnamon stick, 4 inches long
9 fresh hierba santa leaves, or ½ cup fresh epazote or cilantro, or ¼ cup dried epazote

Wash and dry the guajillo chiles, and sauté briefly in hot oil over medium heat. Remove from the oil, place in a bowl, and cover with water for ½ hour. Purée in a blender with about 1 cup of the soaking water, and strain. Set aside.

While the chiles are soaking, roast the onions, garlic, tomatillos, tomatoes, cloves, and cinnamon in a dry skillet over medium heat. When the vegetables are scorched and the spices are warm, blend with the hierba santa, oregano, peanuts, and ½ cup water; strain and set aside.

Heat ½ cup oil in a 2-quart saucepan. Sauté the ¼ onion until black, remove the onion, and discard. Remove the saucepan from the heat. Add the puréed chiles to the oil, and stir. Add the roasted, puréed vegetables and spices, and stir to mix. Return to the heat and cook over low heat for 1 hour.

Combine the masa with the vegetable broth, add salt to taste, and add to the sauce. Cook over low heat for ½ hour, being careful not to let it stick on the bottom!

While the mole sauce is cooking, form the chochoyones (corn dumplings). They will be served with the mole. To make them, mix the 1½ cups masa, vegetable stock, oil, and salt. Knead on a table or counter for about 5-10 minutes until the masa obtains a silky texture and no longer sticks to the fingers. Form this dough into balls the size of a large marble, and form an indentation in each one by pressing it with the thumb or forefinger.

Check the mole. It should be the consistency of a thick soup. If it is thicker than this, add sufficient water to thin it. When the mole is gently bubbling, add the chochoyones, and cook over low heat for 20 minutes. While the chochoyones are cooking, heat the butter in a large skillet. Add the halved chayotes and green beans, cover, and reduce the heat. Cook on low heat for 10 minutes. Serve ½ chayote on each plate, flat side down, with green beans surrounding it. Ladle hot mole sauce, with chochoyones, over these, and garnish with the chopped scallions. Serve with Mexican Rice (page 128) and soft, hot tortillas.

Per serving: Calories: 378, Protein: 5 gm., Fat: 29 gm., Carbohydrates: 22 gm.

1 teaspoon oregano, dried, or 3 teaspoons fresh
½ cup peanuts, roasted
2 cups water
½ cup vegetable oil
¼ medium onion, not separated
½ cup fresh corn dough (masa)
4 cups vegetable stock or water
salt to taste
½ cup butter
6 chayotes, boiled 20 minutes, peeled, and cut in half, or zucchini
1 pound green beans, cut in half and boiled 5 minutes
1 cup scallions, finely chopped
Chochoyones (corn dumplings):
1½ cups fresh masa
6 tablespoons vegetable stock or water
3 tablespoons oil
1 teaspoon fine sea salt

Baby in a Blanket

(Vegetable Strudel)

Niño Envuelto

Serves 4-5
Preparation time: 15 minutes
Cooking time: 30 minutes

½ pound spinach
2 tablespoons onion, chopped
½ teaspoon finely ground sea
  salt
¼ teaspoon grated nutmeg
½ pound grated white cheese
  (use one that melts nicely, such
  as Gruyere or Muenster)
⅔ pound Flaky Pastry Dough
  (page 163)

These vegetable strudels are very popular at La Casa del Pan. Jody Randall showed me how to make the spinach-cheese strudel variation below.

Steam the spinach and onions for 5 minutes, and squeeze out any excess liquid. Preheat the oven to 350°F. Combine the spinach, salt, nutmeg, and cheese.

Roll out the dough into an 8 x 15-inch rectangle. Arrange the spinach-cheese mixture in a lengthwise strip across the dough, near the edge closest to you (but not on it). Fold the edge over to cover the mixture. Carefully roll up the strudel with the filling inside. Pinch the ends together, so that no filling can come out. Transfer the roll to a lightly oiled cookie sheet, and bake for about 30 minutes, or until golden brown.

Per serving: Calories: 547, Protein: 19 gm., Fat: 34 gm., Carbohydrates: 37 gm.

Variations: Instead of spinach, prepare ½ pound of the following: sautéed onions with strips of poblano chile and corn kernels, sautéed onions with strips of nopalito cactus, or steamed Swiss chard with 2 tablespoons chopped onion or mixed vegetables of your own choosing.

Chayotes Stuffed With Cheese

Chayotes Rellenos

Serves 3-4
Preparation time: 20 minutes

The noble chayote grows on a climbing vine, needs no care, returns year after year, and yields a large, edible root as well as green, pear-shaped chayotes and delicious young leaves and runners. Select tender chayotes for this recipe. They are brighter green than more mature fruit, and their skin feels soft. This recipe is an adaptation from San Cristobal de las Casas, where we first tried our cook Maria Luisa's version of it in 1970. The green tomatillo sauce is a later addition.

Boil the whole chayotes in salted water until tender, approximately 20-30 minutes, then cool. Meanwhile, in another pot, boil all the ingredients for the sauce for 15 minutes, and blend. Combine the oregano, thyme, ¼ teaspoon salt, and the pepper. Slice the chayotes lengthwise in 4 slices each. Place a slice of cheese between each pair of slices, and press together. Heat the oil in a large skillet. Beat the egg yolks and add the flour, and seasonings. Dip the cheese-stuffed chayotes into the egg, and coat with the bread crumbs, cheese, and herb mixture. Bake at 350°F until golden brown. Serve with the heated tomatillo sauce poured over each one.

Per serving: Calories: 311, Protein: 17 gm., Fat: 13 gm., Carbohydrates: 29 gm.

3 chayotes
¼ lb. Jack cheese, thinly sliced
1 egg, beaten slightly
½ cup whole wheat bread crumbs
¼ cup parmesan cheese, grated
¼ teaspoon oregano
¼ teaspoon thyme
¼ teaspoon salt
⅛ teaspoon pepper
sauce:
3 cloves garlic, peeled
1 medium onion, sliced
3 green chiles (jalapeno or serrano), seeded and deveined
2 cups tomatillos
3 tablespoons fresh cilantro
¼ teaspoon sea salt
water

House Tostadas

Tostadas De La Casa

Serves 6
Preparation time: 25 minutes

12 corn tortillas
¼ cup vegetable oil for frying
1 medium red or yellow onion,
   sliced
2 cups cabbage, shredded
1 teaspoon oregano
sea salt to taste
1½ cups refried beans
2 cups shredded iceberg lettuce
1 cup avocado, mashed
juice of 1 lime
sea salt to taste
1 cup natural, unflavored yogurt
1 cup Fresh Mexican Chile Sauce
   (page 142) or Guadalajara Hot
   Sauce (page 143) or other salsa

Variation:
1 cup textured vegetable protein
   granules
⅞ cup hot water
½ teaspoon ground cumin
   (optional)

This recipe is very popular at La Casa del Pan. These are hearty tostadas.

In a small skillet, fry the tortillas in the oil on both sides one at a time until crisp. You can also bake these in a 400°F oven for 3 minutes, using only 2 tablespoons oil. Drain on paper. In the oil that remains, fry the onion over medium heat for 5 minutes. Add the cabbage and continue to fry, stirring occasionally, for 5 minutes. Add the oregano and salt. Cover, and lower the heat. Simmer for 10 minutes. Meanwhile, spread the refried beans thinly on the crisp tortillas. Prepare the avocado by mashing it with a fork and adding the juice of 1 lime and salt to taste. Place a portion of the cooked cabbage on each tortilla (tostada) on top of the refried beans. Cover this with shredded lettuce, the avocado (just a spoonful is enough), a spoonful of yogurt, and a spoonful of salsa.

Per serving: Calories: 428, Protein: 11 gm., Fat: 20 gm., Carbohydrates: 49 gm.

Variation: *Textured Vegetable Protein Tostadas*
Here's a delicious way to prepare high-protein textured vegetable protein.

Follow the recipe for House Tostadas de la Casa, but substitute the textured vegetable protein for the cabbage. Mix the textured vegetable protein with the hot water, soak for 10 minutes, and sauté with the onion, salt, oregano, and cumin.

Per serving: Calories: 466, Protein: 17 gm., Fat: 21 gm., Carbohydrates: 52 gm.

Chipotle Dumplings

Albondigas con Chipotle

Here is a textured vegetable protein dumpling recipe, transformed from a Mexican recipe with Moorish influence.

Serves 6-8
Preparation time: 45 minutes

Combine the textured vegetable protein granules with the hot water, and soak for 10 minutes. Combine with the flour, onion, oregano, salt, and black pepper. Use 1 tablespoon at a time, and shape the textured vegetable mixture into balls. Sauté in the oil for 10 minutes, turning to brown evenly. Drain on paper towels.

Prepare the sauce by sautéing the chiles and onions in the oil. Add the tomatoes and sauté until the tomatoes dissolve. Add the vegetable stock, garlic, and epazote. Simmer for 15 minutes, blend, and strain. Return to the heat and add the textured vegetable protein albondigas. Simmer for 10 minutes more, and serve with Mexican Rice with Vegetables (page 128), beans, and a salad.

Per serving: Calories: 242, Protein: 13 gm., Fat: 12 gm., Carbohydrates: 20 gm.

2 cups textured vegetable protein granules
1¾ cups hot water
½ cup flour
1 onion, finely chopped
2 teaspoons oregano
½ teaspoon sea salt
¼ teaspoon freshly ground black pepper
¼ cup sesame oil
sauce:
1-6 chipotle chiles, dried or canned (depending on how spicy you want it)
2 ancho chiles
2 medium onions, sliced
2 tablespoons sesame oil
6 large tomatoes, peeled and chopped
1 cup Vegetable Stock (page 34) or water
½ whole head garlic
1 sprig fresh epazote, or
   1 teaspoon dried epazote or

Stuffed Cabbage in Chipotle Sauce

Repollo Relleno en Salsa de Chipotle

Serves 4-5
Preparation time: 20 minutes
Cooking time: 20 minutes

Cabbage is sold in huge quantities in the San Cristobal market by the Chamula Indians, many of whom carry it to San Cristobal in net bags suspended by "tump-lines" from their foreheads. It's a nutritious, cancer-preventing vegetable. This recipe is an invention of La Casa del Pan, using locally-available ingredients.

Cabbage Rolls:
1 head of cabbage
2 cups cooked rice
1 tablespoon garlic, chopped
¼ cup almonds, blanched and peeled
¼ cup sliced green olives
¼ cup parsley, chopped
1 teaspoon thyme
¼ cup chopped zucchini
sea salt to taste
Chipotle Sauce:
4 medium tomatoes, roasted
3 chipotle chiles, seeded and washed
2 cloves of garlic
salt to taste

Remove the center core and outer leaves from 1 head of cabbage, and drop it into boiling water. Lift out after a few minutes, and remove the soft leaves. Repeat, immersing the head and removing leaves until you have separated 12 of them.

In a large bowl, mix the rice, garlic, almonds, olives, parsley, thyme, zucchini, and salt. Put a portion of this mixture into the middle of each cabbage leaf, fold the sides over, and then roll up into a packet. Arrange in a greased baking pan, and set aside. Preheat the oven to 375°F.

To prepare the sauce, put the tomatoes, chiles, and garlic in a blender, purée, and strain. Add the salt to taste. Pour the sauce over the cabbage rolls, cover, and bake, for 20 minutes.

Per serving: Calories: 245, Protein: 6 gm., Fat: 6 gm., Carbohydrates: 42 gm.

Flower Balls

Albondigas de Flor de Colorín

Don't miss trying this recipe! It is exquisite. Mexico has many edible flowers which also grow in California, and other southern and southwestern states of the U.S. The flower that is prepared in this recipe has petals shaped like small scarlet sabers. They bloom on the colorín (a leguminous tree) before the leaves begin to come out in the early spring. These flowers are never sold in supermarkets, nor even in farmer's markets, but are collected from the trees themselves. Collecting food in the wild is a very joyous experience!

Serves 4
Preparation time: 45 minutes
Cooking time: 25 minutes

4 cups of colorín or chrysanthemum petals
1 tablespoon fresh garlic, minced
1 tablespoon onion, minced
1 tablespoon fresh thyme, chopped or ½ teaspoon dried
1 cup seasoned whole wheat or rye bread crumbs
½ cup sunflower oil
3 eggs, separated
½ teaspoon salt

Clean the flowers by pulling the straw-like pistil out from the bottom. (To do this, pinch the base of the petal as you gently pull on the top with your other hand.) Boil in salted water for 15 minutes, then drain. Mix the garlic, onion, and thyme, then chop the colorín petals and add to the mixture. When these are well-mixed, take small handfuls, and form into balls, squeezing tightly. Cover with bread crumbs.

Heat the oil in a heavy saucepan over medium heat. Beat the egg whites with ½ teaspoon salt until stiff but not dry. Beat the yolks with a fork, and fold them into the whites. Dip the individual flower balls into the egg, and place in the oil. Deep-fry until crispy, turning to brown all sides. Place on paper towels to drain. Dip them in warm Mild or Hot Ranchero Sauce (pages 146, 147) as an appetizer, or serve with Ranchero Sauce as a main dish. Your guests will love you for your efforts.

Per serving: Calories: 220, Protein: 6 gm., Fat: 15 gm., Carbohydrates: 8 gm.

Beans

Frijoles

Beans Boiled in a Pot

Frijoles de Olla

The secret of delicious Mexican beans lies in their freshness and how they are boiled. Fresh beans are shiny and plump. Everyone in Mexico, from all walks of life, eats beans. In peasant homes, they are boiled in a clay pot placed next to the fire in the middle of the dirt floor of the wattle and daub or adobe cottage. In the city, they are cooked on stoves in enamel pots with lids or sometimes in pressure cookers. Having tried the whole range of beans in generous households across the country for over 25 years, I think the best beans are those that are slowly boiled in an earthenware pot. If you don't have a Mexican earthenware bean pot that narrows at the neck to reduce the evaporation rate, the next best thing is a crock-pot. Diane Kennedy, a well-known authority on Mexican cooking, recommends starting the beans with hot water for best results. I have seen peasant women use this method. All of the water they add during cooking, which can take up to 4 hours, is hot water. I don't know of any Mexican cooks who soak beans before boiling them, although this can significantly reduce the cooking time.

Serves 10
Preparation time: 10 minutes
Cooking time 3 to 4 hours

1 pound beans (black, red, or pinto)
3 quarts water
1 small onion, quartered
1 tablespoon coarse, unrefined sea salt
1 large sprig epazote (for black beans)

Per serving: Calories: 65, Protein: 3 gm., Fat: 0 gm., Carbohydrates: 12 gm.

Remove any rocks or sticks from the beans, and rinse. Place the beans in an unglazed, earthenware pot or crock-pot. Cover with hot water, bring to a boil, and reduce to a simmer. Cook slowly for 2 hours, adding more hot water as necessary.

Add the onion and salt. If you are cooking black beans, add the epazote for the last ½ hour of cooking, when the beans are barely tender, but the broth is not yet thick. Stir the bottom with a wooden spoon to prevent sticking. Serve in bowls with warm tortillas wrapped in a cotton napkin and some pickled chiles on the side.

Black Beans Jarocho-Style

Frijoles Jarocho

Beans, combined with corn tortillas, provide high-quality complete protein and high fiber to your diet. Cook the beans until they smash easily, and serve with Fresh Mexican Chile Sauce (page 142) and soft, hot corn tortillas.

In an earthenware pot, cover the beans with hot water. Bring to a boil, reduce the heat, and cook for 2 hours. Add the remaining ingredients and boil until soft, about 1 to 2 more hours.

Per serving: Calories: 72, Protein: 4 gm., Fat: 0 gm., Carbohydrates: 14 gm.

Serves 10
Preparation time: 5 minutes
Cooking time: 3 to 4 hours

1 pound black beans (choose freshly-dried, black shiny beans)
3 quarts hot water
1 whole head fresh garlic
2 chipotle chiles
2-3 sprigs fresh epazote
1 medium onion, sliced
coarse sea salt to taste

Refried Beans

Frijoles Refritos

Although any leftover beans may be used for this recipe, the traditional ones are the Beans Boiled in a Pot (page 122) or Black Beans Jarocho-Style (page 123).

Heat the oil in a skillet, and add the onion. Sauté until the onion is black, then remove form the skillet. Take the skillet from the heat, add the blended beans, and return to the stove. Cook over very low heat, stirring until thickened as desired.

Per serving: Calories: 198, Protein: 7 gm., Fat: 9 gm., Carbohydrates: 22 gm.

Serves 6
Preparation time: 5 minutes
Cooking time: 15 to 20 minutes

¼ cup sunflower oil
½ medium onion, sliced
3 cups cooked beans, blended with their liquid

Crusty Buns with Refried Beans and Melted Cheese

Molletes

Serves 2
Preparation time: 5 minutes
Cooking time: 4 minutes

2 crusty bolillos, or 1 mini-baguette, sliced in half lengthwise
⅔ cup Colby, Jack, or muenster cheese, grated
⅔ cup Refried Beans (page 123)
garnish:
½ cup plain unsweetened yogurt or sour cream
½ cup Fresh Mexican Chile Sauce (page 142)

These open-faced, broiled cheese-and-refried-bean sandwiches are popular in Mexico, where they are offered in many restaurants. A 12-year-old can prepare them in 10 minutes, if the ingredients are on hand.

Preheat the broiler. Spread the refried beans evenly on each of the 4 halves of the bolillos. Sprinkle the cheese on top, and place on a cookie sheet under the broiler until the cheese melts, about 3 to 4 minutes. Serve with yogurt or sour cream and Fresh Mexican Chile Sauce.

Per serving: Calories: 446, Protein: 22 gm., Fat: 19 gm., Carbohydrates: 45 gm.

Tortillas in Bean Sauce

Enfrijoladas

This is a down-home recipe you won't find on restaurant menus, but is popular with Mexicans at family meal times. It is quick, easy, and good, and a favorite with hungry children.

Mix the beans and water, and heat over medium heat. Soften the tortillas by warming them one by one on a heated skillet or griddle. Dip each tortilla in the bean sauce, then place on a plate, put a portion of grated cheese on one half, and fold the other half over. These can go directly to the table or into the oven for gentle heating.

Per serving: Calories: 333, Protein: 15 gm., Fat: 15 gm., Carbohydrates: 35 gm.

Serves 4
Preparation time: 5 minutes
Cooking time: 3 minutes

1 cup refried beans
½ cup water
8 tortillas
1 cup Chihuahua or Jack cheese, grated

White Beans with Ancho Chiles

Alubias con Chiles Anchos

This is a special bean dish which uses alubias, (white navy beans). Originally from northern Mexico, it is served in the south as well.

Soak the ancho chiles in warm water for 5 minutes, and remove the seeds and veins. Cook the beans with all the ingredients, adding water if necessary, until the beans are tender. Remember, the longer they are cooked, the thicker the sauce becomes. Serve with heated flour tortillas wrapped in a cotton napkin.

Per serving: Calories: 139, Protein: 7 gm., Fat: 0 gm., Carbohydrates: 27 gm.

Serves 8-10
Preparation time: 15 minutes
Cooking time: 2-3 hours

6 ancho chiles
1 pound white beans
3 quarts water
2 onions, sliced
1 whole head of garlic
sea salt to taste

Bean Burritos

Burritos

Serves 6
Preparation time: 10 minutes

If you have the ingredients leftover from previous Mexican meals, this recipe can be made, eaten, and cleaned up in half an hour.

2 cups refried beans
6 large whole wheat tortillas
½ cup Mild or Hot Ranchero Sauce (pages 146, 147) or Fresh Mexican Chile Sauce (page 142)
⅔ cup yogurt
¼ cup green onion, chopped
lettuce, shredded
Jack cheese, grated (optional)

Heat the beans. Heat the tortillas one by one on a comal, pancake griddle, or dry skillet. Place a row of beans across the middle of each tortilla, and roll into a cylinder. Serve accompanied by a sauce, the yogurt, green onion, lettuce, and cheese.

Per serving: Calories: 236, Protein: 8 gm., Fat: 8 gm., Carbohydrates: 32 gm.

Side Dishes

Platillos Para Acompanar

Mexican Rice with Vegetables

Arroz a La Mexicana

Serves 10
Preparation time: 10 minutes
Cooking time: 20 minutes

½ cup sunflower oil
1 clove garlic
3 cups (2 pounds) rice
1 onion, sliced
2 small tomatoes, peeled, seeded,
   and chopped
1 poblano chile, cut in strips
1 medium zucchini, cut in strips
2 carrots, cut in strips
1 chayote, cut in strips, or
   ½ cup peas
4 cups hot water
salt to taste
1 teaspoon pepper
1 sprig fresh thyme

This recipe is from Reina, my cook from La Casa del Pan. She uses white rice, which is traditional. If you want to substitute brown rice, use ½ cup more water, cook for 35 minutes, and allow to stand covered for 5 minutes before serving.

Heat the oil in a 1½-quart pot with a tight-fitting lid. Brown the garlic and rice for about 15 minutes. Add the onion and tomatoes, and brown with the rice for 5 more minutes. Add the chile, zucchini, carrots, and chayote, and brown for 2 more minutes. Add the water, salt, black pepper, and thyme, and bring to a boil. Lower the heat, cover with a tight-fitting lid, and simmer for another 20 minutes.

Per serving: Calories: 170, Protein: 2 gm., Fat: 10 gm., Carbohydrates: 16 gm.

Jarocho Rice

Arroz Jarocho

If you time the rice to a well-sung "Son Jarocho" from Veracruz, it will come out just right. If you dance to the music, you will no longer need to pay to drive through traffic to aerobics class. If you sing with the musicians, you will learn endless spontaneous erotic puns. And if you dance AND sing while your rice cooks, you will be in heaven on earth.

Servings: 8 hungry people
Preparation time: 20 minutes
Cooking time: 20 to 35 minutes

Sauté the onion and garlic in the oil over medium heat for 5 minutes, stirring occasionally. Add the rice and sauté for about 15 minutes. Then add the remaining ingredients, and bring to a boil. Reduce the heat to low, cover with a tight-fitting lid, and dance 20 minutes for white rice, or 35 minutes for brown rice.

Per serving: Calories: 277, Protein: 4 gm., Fat: 7 gm., Carbohydrates: 49 gm.

½ onion, sliced
½ head of garlic, peeled and minced
¼ cup olive oil
2 cups white or brown rice, washed and drained
4½ cups water or vegetable stock
½ cup raisins
2 plantains or bananas, sliced
1 teaspoon sea salt

Chayotes with Mint

Chayotes con Menta

Serves 4
Preparation time: 5 minutes
Cooking time: 15 to 25 minutes

4 small or 2 medium chayotes,
  peeled and coarsely chopped
½ cup water
½ teaspoon sea salt
2 tablespoons fresh mint, finely
  chopped
2 tablespoons butter
freshly ground black pepper to
  taste

Select tender young chayotes for this aromatic recipe that melts in your mouth.

In a 2-quart saucepan, heat the chayotes in the water with the salt, until the water boils. Cover and cook for 15 to 25 minutes until tender. Pour off the water, and toss the chayotes with the mint, butter, and pepper. Serve hot.

Per serving: Calories: 70, Protein: 1 gm., Fat: 6 gm., Carbohydrates: 3 gm.

San Cristobal Chipilín Rice

Arroz con Chipilín

Serves 8
Preparation time: 15 minutes
Cooking time: 35 minutes

6 cloves garlic, chopped
½ cup sesame oil
2 cups brown rice
5 cups water
1 cup chipilín leaves, cilantro, or
  parsley, chopped
1½ teaspoons sea salt

Chipilín is a flavorful herb found in southern Mexico. Outside of that area, it is difficult to find, so you'll have to use a substitute for it, unless you are lucky enough to be living or travelling in the area. I recommend cilantro, but parsley may also be used.

Sauté the garlic in the oil for 5 minutes, stirring occasionally. Add the rice, and continue to sauté, stirring occasionally, for 10 minutes. Add the water, chipilín, and salt, cover, and lower the heat to the minimum. Cook until the rice is tender and has consumed all the water, about 35 minutes.

Per serving: Calories: 267, Protein: 3 gm., Fat: 13 gm., Carbohydrates: 32 gm.

Colache

If accompanied with beans on the side, this dish, including its name, is right out of a pre-Hispanic milpa (a cornfield consisting of corn, beans, squash, peppers, and greens).

In a 2-quart saucepan, heat the oil and sauté the green onions and poblano chile for 5 minutes. Add the tomatoes and cook, stirring, for 5 more minutes. Add the zucchini, yellow squash, cilantro or epazote, sweet corn kernels, salt, and pequín chile, and cover. Lower the heat, and cook for 5 more minutes, or until the vegetables are barely tender. Serve with beans and rice.

Per serving: Calories: 132, Protein: 2 gm., Fat: 5 gm., Carbohydrates: 17 gm.

Serves 4-6
Preparation time: 15 minutes
Cooking time: 15 minutes

2 tablespoons corn oil
3 green onions, chopped
1 poblano chile, stem removed, seeded, and chopped
½ pound tomatoes, peeled, seeded, and chopped
1 pound zucchini, chopped
½ pound yellow squash, chopped
1 sprig fresh cilantro or epazote
kernels from 4 ears of fresh sweet corn
1 teaspoon sea salt
pinch of ground pequín chile

Boiled Corn on the Cob

Elotes Hervidos

Serves 8
Preparation time: 15 minutes

8 ears of sweet corn, husked
3 quarts boiling water, salted
½ cup mayonnaise
½ cup Jack cheese, grated
1 teaspoon ground pequín chile
1 teaspoon fine sea salt

Here are a couple of ways to prepare corn on the cob as it is sold by the street vendors throughout Mexico.

Boil the corn until tender, about 10 minutes. Pierce each ear at the base with a pointed stick or corn fork. Smear with mayonnaise, roll in the grated cheese, and sprinkle with a mixture of ground chile and salt.

Per serving: Calories: 131, Protein: 3 gm., Fat: 6 gm., Carbohydrates: 15 gm.

Roasted Corn on the Cob

Elotes Rotizados

Serves 8
Preparation time: 15 minutes

8 ears of sweet corn, husked
4 fresh limes, cut in half
1 teaspoon ground pequín chile
1 teaspoon fine sea salt

Roast the corn over a charcoal fire or under the broiler, turning until it browns. Pierce through the base of each with a pointed stick or corn fork. Smear with lime juice, squeezed directly onto each ear. Sprinkle with a mixture of chile and salt.

Per serving: Calories: 61, Protein: 1 gm., Fat: 0 gm., Carbohydrates: 13 gm.

Tortillas in Tomato Sauce

Entomatadas

My friend "Magos" (Margarita Sires) shared this tasty and easy recipe with me. Entomatadas means "in tomatoes," and refers to tortillas fried lightly in oil, dipped in tomato sauce, and then covered with cream and cheese. They require only a few minutes to prepare.

Blend the tomatoes, onion, and garlic, and strain. Heat the oil in an 8-inch frying pan, and add the tomato purée. Cook, stirring occasionally, for 10-15 minutes. Add the salt.

In another small frying pan, heat ¼ cup oil, and fry the tortillas one at a time, allowing about 10 seconds per side. Dip each one into the tomato sauce to soften, fold in half, and remove to a hot plate. Arrange three on each plate, and cover with the sour cream, cheese, and scallions. Serve with refried beans and a tossed green salad.

Per serving: Calories: 344, Protein: 8 gm., Fat: 24 gm., Carbohydrates: 24 gm.

Serves 4
Preparation time: 10 minutes
Cooking time: 15 minutes

½ **pound tomatoes**
½ **onion**
1 **clove garlic**
2 **tablespoons sunflower oil**
½ **teaspoon salt**
¼ **cup sunflower oil, for frying**
6 **corn tortillas**
½ **cup sour cream (the most natural you can find), or plain, unsweetened yogurt**
½ **cup Chihuahua or other white cheese, grated**
4 **scallions, chopped**

Masa Patties from Piedras Negras

Tortitas de Piedras Negras

Makes 20 balls
Preparation time: 10 minutes
Cooking time: 15 minutes

Piedras Negras means "black rocks" and is the name of a town in northern Mexico. This family recipe was given to me by Angelica Inda. The only change is the substitution of butter for lard. You can also use vegetable oil.

1 ancho chile, well soaked in
   ¼ cup hot water
1 pound freshly made tortilla
   dough
2 tablespoons butter or vegetable
   oil
2 ounces Chihuahua cheese
salt to taste
2 to 4 tablespoons corn oil for
   frying
½ cup Hot Ranchero Sauce
   (page 147)
½ cup Chihuahua cheese, grated
   (optional)

Pulverize the ancho chile with the soaking water in a blender. Mix the dough with the butter, and add the ancho chile purée, 2 ounces of cheese, and salt. Knead until these ingredients are well blended. Form balls the size of a ping pong ball, and flatten between your palms. Fry in a nonstick pan in the corn oil, and drain. Serve with Hot Ranchero Sauce for dipping, or accompany the tortitas with black beans and a tossed salad to make a meal.

Per ball: Calories: 86, Protein: 2 gm., Fat: 4 gm., Carbohydrates: 10 gm.

Green Rice with Chiles

Arroz Verde con Rajas

This rice makes a beautiful dish to serve as a buffet. It is mildly spicy. To take the bite out of the chiles, peel them and soak in salted water for 15 minutes.

Serves 8
Preparation time: 15 minutes
Cooking time: 40 minutes

Rinse the rice and drain in a colander. Blend the spinach, parsley, onion, and garlic with ½ cup cold water, and set aside. In a 1½-quart saucepan with a tight-fitting lid, heat the oil and sauté the rice for 10 minutes over medium heat, stirring frequently. Drain off the excess oil, add the hot water and spinach mixture, and season with salt. Lower the heat, cover, and cook 40 minutes.

While the rice is cooking, prepare the garnish by heating the butter in a 1-quart saucepan, and sautéing the onions for 5 minutes, stirring frequently. Add the poblano chiles, sauté for 15 more minutes, and set aside. When the rice is done, place it in a buttered casserole dish, and cover it first with the chiles and then with the grated cheese. Cover with a lid or aluminum foil. Warm it in a preheated 350°F oven for 20 minutes before serving.

Per serving: Calories: 268, Protein: 7 gm., Fat: 14 gm., Carbohydrates: 28 gm.

2 cups brown rice
2 cups spinach, chopped
1 cup parsley, chopped
½ medium onion, chopped
2 cloves garlic, peeled and chopped
½ cup cold water
½ cup vegetable oil
4 cups hot water
1 teaspoon sea salt, or to taste
garnish:
2 tablespoons butter
1 pound onions, thinly sliced
4 large poblano chiles, roasted, peeled, deveined, seeded, and cut in strips
1 cup Chihuahua or Swiss cheese, grated

Ginger Carrots

Zanahorias con Jenjibre

Serves 6
Preparation time: 10 minutes
Cooking time: 15 minutes

1 pound carrots, peeled and sliced thinly
1 tablespoon gingerroot, freshly grated, or 1 teaspoon ground ginger
¼ cup fresh squeezed orange juice
2 teaspoons honey
½ teaspoon sea salt, or to taste

I recommend fresh ginger for this recipe. In combination with the orange juice and honey, it makes a very aromatic dish. This is fine food to cure a cold.

Combine the carrots and gingerroot in a 2-quart saucepan. Cover with water and cook over medium heat until the carrots are tender, about 15 minutes. Drain, add the orange juice, honey, and salt, and serve.

Per serving: Calories: 92, Protein: 1 gm., Fat: 0 gm., Carbohydrates: 21 gm.

Baked Sweet Potato Pudding

Budin de Camote

Sweet potatoes are a favorite in Mexico, where they are peddled through the streets at night by the street vendors who steam them in homemade ovens on wheels. You can tell when one is nearby from the loud whistle made when the steam is let out. When they hear the whistle, people come out of their homes to buy them, sprinkled with cinnamon, sugar, and moistened with cream.

Serves 4-5
Preparation time: 10 minutes
Cooking time: 45 minutes

Preheat the oven to 350°F. Boil the sweet potatoes in enough water to cover until tender, about 30 minutes. Drain and blend with the sugar, butter, cinnamon, low-fat milk, and sweet cream. Add the orange peel, and place in a buttered casserole. Decorate with half the raisins and pine nuts. Sprinkle the top with 1 tablespoon brown sugar, and bake for 15 minutes. Remove from the oven and decorate with the remaining raisins and pine nuts.

1 pound yellow sweet potatoes
½ cup dark brown sugar
¼ cup butter
1 teaspoon ground cinnamon
½ cup low-fat milk
¼ cup thick, sweet cream
grated peel of one orange
¼ cup golden raisins
¼ cup pine nuts
1 tablespoon dark brown sugar

Per serving: Calories: 431, Protein: 3 gm., Fat: 18 gm., Carbohydrates: 61 gm.

Flor's Sauced Zucchini

Calabacitas de Flor

Serves 6
Preparation time: 10 minutes
Cooking time: 15 minutes

Every time I visit my neighbor Flor, she's either cooking or eating. And she's not fat. Her recipes, which I have been lucky to sample over the years, are low in fat and high in fiber, and they're all delicious. She's from Oaxaca, land of some of Mexico's most delicious cooking.

1 medium onion, chopped
2 tablespoons sunflower oil
4 medium zucchini squash, chopped
2 fresh jalapeño chiles, seeded and chopped
kernels from 3 ears of corn
2 tomatoes, peeled, seeded and chopped
½ teaspoon sea salt, or to taste
½ cup Jack cheese, grated (optional)

Saute the onion in the oil for 3 minutes. Add the zucchini, jalapeño chiles, corn and tomatoes, and cook, stirring, for 3 more minutes. Add the salt and cheese, cover, and cook for 15 more minutes over low heat.

Per serving: Calories: 78, Protein: 2 gm., Fat: 5 gm., Carbohydrates: 8 gm.

Fresh Corn Kernels

Esquites

In Mexico City, you can buy these on street corners served hot in plastic cups, from the women selling boiled corn on the cob.

Sauté the onion and serrano chiles in the oil for 5 minutes, stirring constantly. Add the corn and sauté 3 more minutes. Add the remaining ingredients, cover, and cook over medium heat for 20 more minutes. Serve hot.

Per serving: Calories: 200, Protein: 2 gm., Fat: 9 gm., Carbohydrates: 28 gm.

Serves 6
Preparation time: 15 minutes
Cooking time: 20 minutes

1 cup onion, finely chopped
5 serrano chiles, seeded, and finely chopped
¼ cup corn oil
the kernels from 10 ears of fresh sweet corn
¼ cup fresh epazote or cilantro, chopped
¼ cup fresh parsley, chopped
¾ cup water
1 teaspoon sea salt

Green Beans Supreme

Ejotes Suprema

Serves 6-8
Preparation time: 15 minutes

This is a rich-tasting dish but low in calories. Use the most tender beans you can find.

2 quarts water
½ teaspoon salt
2 pounds tender, fresh green
   beans
2 tablespoons butter
1 medium onion, chopped
½ cup parsley, chopped
2 tablespoons flour
½ teaspoon lime or lemon rind,
   grated
1 teaspoon salt
¼ teaspoon freshly ground
   black pepper
1 cup yogurt
½ cup Parmesan cheese

Bring the 2 quarts of water and salt to a boil. Add the green beans and cook over high heat for 5 minutes; drain and reserve the cooking water. Melt the butter in a wide skillet, and sauté the onion and parsley for 5 minutes. Add the flour and brown 3 minutes. Add ¼ cup of the water in which the beans were cooked, and allow to thicken. Add the beans, lime rind, salt, black pepper, and yogurt, and stir to combine. Transfer to a serving dish, sprinkle with Parmesan cheese, and serve.

Per serving: Calories: 173, Protein: 5 gm., Fat: 11 gm., Carbohydrates: 13 gm.

Sauces and Relishes

Salsas y Encurtidos

Fresh Mexican Chile Sauce

Salsa Mexicana

Serves 4-5 people who like chiles
Preparation time: 5 minutes

**3 tablespoons fresh jalapeño
chiles, finely chopped**
**3 Italian tomatoes, or 2 large
round ones, chopped**
**1 tablespoon fresh cilantro or
parsley, chopped**
juice of 1 lime
**¼ teaspoon finely ground sea
salt**

This is your basic fresh sauce to accompany most Mexican meals. It takes moments to dash up, should always be made fresh, and is always appreciated.

Combine the ingredients and serve.

Per serving: Calories: 22, Protein: 1 gm., Fat: 0 gm., Carbohydrates: 4 gm.

jalapeños

Guadalajara Hot Sauce

Salsa Tapatío

The word tapatio affectionately refers to people from Guadalajara. My friend, Alicia Cardenas de Michel, showed me this recipe to accompany tortas ahogadas (drowned sandwiches) from Guadalajara. It has become a staple in our home, and is one of the canned chile products offered in La Casa del Pan. Careful! This sauce is liquid fire! Mexicans visiting your home will sweat when they eat it.

Serves 10 chile lovers
Preparation time: 10 minutes

8 dried de arbol chiles (or
   any small dried chiles)
3 fat cloves of garlic, peeled
juice of 2 limes
½ teaspoon finely ground sea
   salt, or to taste
spring water

Roast the chiles in a dry skillet over medium heat for 5 minutes with the window open (otherwise the vapors rising from the cooking of hot peppers may irritate your eyes and throat). Grind them with the garlic in a molcajeta (stone mortar and pestle), if you have one, or a blender. Add the lime juice, keep grinding or blending, add the salt, and strain. This may be made ahead of time. It keeps well in sterilized jars in the refrigerator.

Per serving: Calories: 25, Protein: 0 gm., Fat: 0 gm., Carbohydrates: 6 gm.

Green Chile Sauce

Salsa Verde

Makes 3 cups
Preparation time: 15 minutes

This sauce is distinguished by the use of the tomatillo, or green tomato. It is used in Swiss Enchiladas (page 78). This is not an unripe tomato, but a small tomato which grows within a thin husk and is ripe when green.

1 pound tomatillos, husked
3 fresh jalapeño chiles
1 clove garlic
2 cups water
⅓ cup fresh cilantro, chopped
¼ cup onion, chopped
1 teaspoon fine sea salt, or
   to taste

In a 1½-quart saucepan over medium heat, cook the tomatillos, chiles, and garlic in the water for 10 minutes. Drain off most of the excess water, reserving 1 cup. Process or blend the tomatillos, garlic, and chiles with this liquid and the cilantro. Add the onion and salt, and allow to stand ½ hour before serving.

Per 2 tablespoons: Calories: 17, Protein: 1 gm., Fat: 0 gm., Carbohydrates: 3 gm.

Red Enchilada Sauce

Salsa de Chile Guajillo

This sauce is made in Mexico City, Morelos, and Guerrero. It makes a good enchilada sauce.

Roast the chiles on a comal or in a wide, dry skillet. Blend with the tomatoes, garlic, water, and salt. Serve heated.

Per 2 tablespoons: Calories: 18, Protein: 1 gm., Fat: 0 gm., Carbohydrates: 4 gm.

Makes 2 cups
Preparation time: 20 minutes

10 guajillo chiles
**3 Italian tomatoes, roasted,
   peeled, and seeded**
2 cloves garlic
1 cup water
1 teaspoon sea salt, or to taste

Mild Ranchero Sauce

Salsa Ranchera Suave

Makes about 4 cups
Preparation time: 10 minutes
Cooking time: 20 minutes

3 dried huajillo chiles
2 pounds (7 medium) tomatoes
1 onion, sliced
6 cloves garlic, minced
2 tablespoons sesame oil
1 cup water
1 teaspoon sea salt

This sauce is mildly spicy and may also be used for enchiladas. Tomatoes are what distinguish this from enchilada sauce. It keeps well for five days refrigerated and also freezes well.

In a dry skillet, roast the chiles for 3 minutes. Roast the tomatoes, peel, and remove the seeds. Sauté the onion and garlic in the oil for 5 minutes. Blend the tomatoes and chiles with the water, strain through a fine strainer, and add to the onion and garlic. Add the salt, and simmer for 20 minutes on low heat.

Per 2 tablespoons: Calories: 17, Protein: 0 gm., Fat: 0 gm., Carbohydrates: 2 gm.

Hot Ranchero Sauce

Salsa Picante

This is a mildly hot tomato sauce, good for dipping chips, or making "huevos rancheros" (ranch eggs).

Sauté the garlic in the oil. Blend the tomatoes with the chiles, strain them, and add to the garlic. Add the water and salt, and simmer on low heat for 20 minutes.

Per 2 tablespoons: Calories: 21, Protein: 0 gm., Fat: 1 gm., Carbohydrates: 2 gm.

Makes 3 cups
Preparation time: 10 minutes
Cooking time: 20 minutes

5 cloves garlic, minced
2 tablespoons olive oil
7 Italian tomatoes, roasted, peeled, and seeded
3-6 dried de arbol chiles, roasted for 3 minutes in a dry skillet
2 cups water
½ teaspoon salt

Hot Chipotle Sauce

Salsa Chipotle

Makes ¾ cup
Preparation time: 10 minutes
Cooking time: 5 minutes

4 dried chipotle chiles
½ cup hot water
2 cloves garlic
½ teaspoon sea salt
¼ cup apple cider vinegar

Soften the chiles in the water for 5 minutes, then remove the seeds. Grind them in a blender with the soaking water, garlic, salt, and vinegar. Cook for 5 minutes over medium heat.

Per tablespoon: Calories: 8, Protein: 0 gm., Fat: 0 gm., Carbohydrates: 2 gm.

Chipotle Chiles

Chiles Chipotles

Makes 3 quarts
Preparation time: 10 minutes
Cooking time: 15 minutes

1 pound chipotle chiles
2 heads of fresh garlic, separated into cloves but not peeled
½ pound (3 medium) carrots, peeled and sliced diagonally
1½ teaspoons whole cloves
10 bay leaves
2 quarts water + 2 quarts apple cider vinegar
1 tablespoon coarse sea salt
two 4-inch cinnamon sticks
1½ cups brown sugar

These dried, smoked, and pickled jalapeños (chipotle chiles) are sweetly pungent and very spicy. They add delicious flavor to soups, stews, sauces, and dips.

Combine all the ingredients in a 4-quart enamel pot. Bring to a boil, reduce the heat, and simmer for 10 minutes. Can according to the instructions given for Pickled Jalapeños with Vegetables (page 150).

Per ½ cup: Calories: 66, Protein: 0 gm., Fat: 0 gm., Carbohydrates: 16 gm.

Red Mole Sauce

Salsa de Mole

This sauce is delicious with enchiladas.

Makes 2 cups
Preparation time: 20 minutes
Cooking time: 20 minutes

The traditional Mexican way to roast the chiles, tomatoes, and garlic is on a hot comal. You may also roast them in a dry skillet, turning to scorch on all sides. Some American cooks roast them under the broiler in the oven. After roasting, blend all the ingredients, except the oil, with enough water to make a thick sauce. Heat the oil in a heavy saucepan, and add the sauce. Cook 20 minutes, adding water to thin the sauce as desired.

Per 2 tablespoons: Calories: 87, Protein: 2 gm., Fat: 6 gm., Carbohydrates: 6 gm.

4 ancho chiles, roasted and seeded
2 tomatoes, roasted, peeled, and seeded
5 cloves of garlic, roasted and peeled
⅓ cup almonds
⅓ cup peanuts
⅓ cup raisins
1 slice toasted bread
3 green onions, chopped
1 teaspoon sea salt water
¼ cup sesame or corn oil

chiles anchos

Pickled Jalapeños with Vegetables

Chiles en Escabeche

Makes 15 to 20 cups
Preparation time: 2 hours

1 pound tender nopales (cactus pods), cut into ½ x 2-inch pieces
1½ pounds (12) whole jalapeño chiles, with stems
¾ cup corn oil
1 pound onion, sliced
½ pound garlic, separated into cloves but not peeled
1 pound carrots, peeled and sliced diagonally
1 large head cauliflower, cut into florettes
1 quart apple cider vinegar
1 quart spring water
8 bay leaves
1 sprig fresh thyme, or 2 teaspoons dried
1 sprig fresh marjoram, or 2 teaspoons dried
1 tablespoon sea salt
2 tablespoons brown sugar

What I like about this recipe is tasting each different vegetable as it is transformed by the pickled chile. Especially the cactus!

Boil the nopales with 1 tablespoon sea salt in enough water to cover for ½ hour, and drain. Wash the chiles. Heat the oil over medium heat in an 8-quart enamel pot. Add the onion and garlic, and sauté until the onion is translucent. Add the carrots and cauliflower, and cook, stirring occasionally, for 15 minutes. Add the chiles and nopales. Heat the apple cider vinegar and water, and pour over the vegetables. Add the herbs, salt, and brown sugar. Cook over high heat until the carrots are barely tender. Do not over cook or the vegetables will turn mushy.

While the chiles are cooking, prepare to can them by filling wide-mouth canning jars of any size half full with water. Place the jars in a pot with 3-4 inches of water. Place lids lightly over each jar. Cover the pot and boil the jars for 15 to 20 minutes, then reduce the heat to low.

Working carefully using tongs, pull out a jar, grasp it with a pot holder, and pour the hot water back into the pot. Using a wide-mouth funnel and a large spoon, fill the jar with an assortment of steaming chiles and vegetables. Then, using a ladle or cup, fill the jar to ½ inch from the top with vinegar brine. Cover tightly right away.

Per ½ cup: Calories: 88, Protein: 1 gm., Fat: 5 gm., Carbohydrates: 10 gm.

Breads

Pan

King's Day Bread Ring

Rosca de Reyes

Serves 12 (Makes one 18-inch ring)
Preparation time: 1½ hours
Baking time: 30 minutes

This festive sweet bread is traditionally served throughout Mexico on the 6th of January, "Día de los Reyes," or King's Day, the day when the three kings visited the baby Jesus. For this reason, each bread ring contains a hidden surprise: a tiny baby doll, the symbol of the Christ child. Friends and family gather around the ring, and take turns cutting their own piece. Whoever finds the doll should invite the other participants of the King's Day ritual to the fiesta of La Candelaria (Candle-mass, held on the 2nd of February), where tamales are traditionally shared.

1 ounce active dry yeast
½ cup lukewarm water
5 cups flour
½ pound unsalted butter, softened
4 eggs
4 egg yolks
1 cup milk
½ cup light brown sugar
½ teaspoon salt
2 tablespoons agua de azahar or orange blossom tea, or 1 teaspoon orange extract
1 cup candied orange peel, chopped, or 1 tablespoon grated orange or lime rind
1 small porcelain doll

Dissolve the yeast in the water with 2 tablespoons of the flour, and allow to stand until it is foamy. Sift the flour onto a large bread board or into a large mixing bowl. Form a well in the middle, and add half of the butter, the eggs, egg yolks, milk, brown sugar, salt, agua de azahar, and yeast water. Combine all the ingredients and work them together with your hands to form a dough. Knead the dough, adding the remainder of the butter gradually until a smooth dough is obtained. Put the dough in a greased bowl, cover, and allow to rise in a warm place until doubled in volume.

To prepare the decorating dough, beat the butter until creamy, then gradually add the sugar, while continuing to beat the butter. Add the flour, and then set the mixture aside. Preheat the oven to 375°F.

Knead the dough for the bread for 5 minutes to squeeze out any air bubbles. Roll it out on a floured board, forming an 8 x 30-inch rectangle. Sprinkle the candied orange peel over the surface, place the doll on top, and roll up the dough. Place the roll on a large cookie sheet lightly greased with butter, forming a large ring. Cover with a damp cloth, and allow to rise in a warm place until doubled in bulk. Decorate with radiating strips of decorating dough and candied fruit, and paint with the egg white. Bake 30 minutes, or until lightly browned.

Per serving: Calories: 494, Protein: 11 gm., Fat: 25 gm., Carbohydrates: 54 gm.

decorating dough:
⅓ cup butter
½ cup powdered sugar
2 egg yolks
¾ cup flour
decoration:
2 egg whites
2 candied figs, cut into strips
2 candied orange peels, cut into strips

rosca de reyes

Crusty Rolls

Bolillos

Makes 10 to 12 bolillos
Preparation time: 1 hour
Baking time: 25 minutes

1½ tablespoons dry yeast
1 tablespoon brown sugar
2½ cups lukewarm water
2 teaspoons sea salt
2 tablespoons butter
4 cups unbleached all purpose
  flour
2 cups whole wheat flour

These rolls are used all over Mexico to make tortas (the popular sandwich, with a wide range of fillings).

Dissolve the yeast and brown sugar in ½ cup of the water, and let stand for 5 minutes. Add the rest of the water, the salt, butter, 2 cups unbleached flour, and 1 cup whole wheat flour. Stir to combine, form into a ball, and knead on a board dusted with some of the remaining flour. Knead for 15 minutes, adding the remaining flour gradually until the dough becomes smooth. Cover with a damp cloth, and allow to rise in a warm place (in a sunny window or equivalent, but not too hot, or it will spoil) until doubled in bulk. Divide into balls about ½ cup in size (3 ounces). Preheat the oven to 375°F. Shape into footballs and place on a lightly greased cookie sheet to rise until doubled in bulk. Slash them across the top with a sharp knife to a depth of about ½ inch. Bake until they begin to brown, about 25 minutes.

Per roll: Calories: 245, Protein: 8 gm., Fat: 3 gm., Carbohydrates: 47 gm.

Pambazos from Jalapa

These tiny buns (2 inches in diameter) are served sliced in half and filled with refried beans and a variety of traditional stews in Jalapa, the capitol of Veracruz. I suggest using refried beans, avocado, onion, shredded lettuce, and chile sauce. Serve them as an appetizer.

Makes 40 bite-size buns
Preparation time: 1 hour
Baking time: 15 to 20 minutes

Dissolve the yeast in the water with a pinch of sugar, allowing it to stand 5 minutes. Add 1 cup of the flour and stir. Allow to stand 15 minutes. Place 1 cup of the flour in a mixing bowl, make a well in the middle, and add the yeast mixture, butter, and salt. Mix, adding water as needed to form the dough into a ball. Knead the dough on a board sprinkled with some of the remaining flour until a silky dough is obtained. Be careful not to add too much flour, or the pambazos will be dry and hard. Cover with a damp cloth, and allow to rise in a warm place (a sunny window, for example) until it has doubled in bulk. This usually takes about 30 minutes. Preheat the oven to 375°F. Form into balls using ¼ cup dough, and place on a lightly greased cookie sheet. Allow to rise, covered with a damp cloth, until doubled in bulk (about 15 minutes). Bake until the buns just begin to brown (about 20 minutes).

**2 tablespoons dry yeast, or
   1 package
1 cup lukewarm water
pinch of sugar
3 cups unbleached white flour
3 cups whole wheat flour
1½ ounces soft butter
1½ teaspoons sea salt**

Per bun: Calories: 69, Protein: 2 gm., Fat: 1 gm., Carbohydrates: 13 gm.

Bread for the Day of the Dead (Nov. 1st)

Pan de Muertos

Makes 5 small loaves
Serves 15

Preparation time: 1½ hours
Baking time: 35-40 minutes

On October 31st of every year, in every household in Mexico, the family altar is decorated with masses of marigolds, photographs and momentos of the family's deceased, and food: mole (ancho chile with chocolate sauce), arroz (rice), frijoles (beans), fruit, chocolate, bread, and whatever specialties the deceased once favored. Throughout Mexico, a special bread is prepared for this offering to the spirits of the departed loved ones. Shaped in a round loaf, decorated with "bones" made of dough, and sprinkled with sugar, it makes a beautiful sight. On the first (or second) day of November, after the essence of the food has been consumed by the spirits, the family carries the food to the cemetery, where they enjoy a picnic at the graves of their loved ones. Consciousness and acceptance of death in a positive way is part of the Mexican culture, and perhaps explains much of the Mexicans' philosophy of life, enjoying the moment. This recipe is the traditional one we prepare at La Casa del Pan.

2 tablespoons dry yeast
½ cup lukewarm water
2 tablespoons brown sugar
2½ pounds flour (I use half whole wheat, half white for this recipe)
1 cup cream or yogurt
4 eggs
2 egg yolks
½ pound unsalted butter

Dissolve the yeast in the water with the sugar, and allow to stand 10 minutes. Mound the flour on a bread board or in a large mixing bowl. Make a well in the middle, and add the cream, eggs, egg yolks, butter, orange rind, and milk. Mix with your hands and form into a ball. Knead energetically on a lightly floured surface until the dough is smooth (about 15 minutes). (Traditional recipes recommend beating the dough against the table.) Cover with a damp cloth and allow to rise in a warm place until doubled in bulk. Knead the dough again, banging it on the table occasionally to remove the excess air. Divide it into 6 equal parts, 5 for shaping into round loaves, and the sixth for shaping into crossed "bones" to place on top of each of the loaves. When the loaves are formed and decorated, place them on cookie sheets, cover, and allow to rise until double in size. Preheat the oven to 375°F. When the loaves have doubled in volume, brush them with the beaten egg, and sprinkle them with sugar. Bake them for about 35 to 40 minutes, or until golden brown.

Per serving: Calories: 422, Protein: 13 gm., Fat: 16 gm., Carbohydrates: 56 gm.

the rind of one small orange, grated
½ quart milk
1 egg, beaten
sugar for decorating

pan de muertos

Whole Wheat Buns

Semitas Chichimecas

Makes 20 small buns

Preparation time: 1½ hours
Baking time: 25 minutes

1 package active dry yeast
½ cup lukewarm water
1 tablespoon brown sugar
5 cups whole wheat flour,
    finely ground
10 tablespoons butter
1⅛ cups dark brown sugar
5 eggs
2 cups lukewarm water
½ teaspoon salt
1 teaspoon powdered cinnamon
1 teaspoon ground anis

This recipe dates from early colonial times. It is still a popular traditional bread in the villages in central and southern Mexico. The traditional pork lard is replaced with butter in this recipe.

Dissolve the yeast in ½ cup lukewarm water with 1 tablespoon brown sugar. Allow to stand 10 minutes, or until the mixture is foamy. Place the flour in a mound on a large bread board or in a large mixing bowl. Make a well in the middle, add the rest of the ingredients, and work them in with your hands. Form a ball with the dough, and knead it for about 10 minutes, adding more flour or water as necessary to form the proper consistency. (The dough should neither be sticky nor too dry.) Cover it with a damp cloth, and allow it to rise in a warm place until it has doubled in volume (about 1 hour). Preheat the oven to 375°F. Divide the dough in 20 equal balls. Arrange on a lightly greased cookie sheet, cover, and allow to rise until doubled in size. Brush with melted butter, sprinkle with sugar, and bake for about 25 minutes or until lightly browned.

Per serving: Calories: 213, Protein: 5 gm., Fat: 8 gm., Carbohydrates: 30 gm.

Chile Corn Bread

This recipe is adapted from a recipe from the American southwest.

Serves 8
Preparation time: 20 minutes
Baking time: 30 minutes

Preheat the oven to 375°F. Combine the cornmeal, salt, and baking powder. Add the corn and yogurt, and stir. Add the oil and eggs, and stir to combine. In a greased, 9-inch square baking dish, spread the onion and chiles evenly. Sprinkle with half of the cheese. Pour the cornmeal batter over them, and cover with the remaining cheese. Bake for 30 minutes or until done.

Per serving: Calories: 302 , Protein: 13 gm., Fat: 16 gm., Carbohydrates: 22 gm.

1 cup cornmeal
1 teaspoon salt
1 tablespoon baking powder
kernels from 3 ears of corn,
   boiled 5 minutes in salted
   water
1 cup unflavored yogurt
   or sour cream
¼ cup corn oil
2 eggs, beaten
1 red onion, chopped
3 poblano chiles, peeled, seeded,
   and chopped
1 cup Chihuahua or Swiss
   cheese, grated
1 cup cheddar cheese, grated

Amaranth Pancakes

Hotcakes de Amaranto

Serves 4
Preparation time: 10 minutes
Cooking time: 5 minutes

dry mixture:
1 cup whole wheat pastry flour
½ cup amaranth flour
1 teaspoon fine sea salt
2 teaspoons baking powder
4 tablespoons brown sugar
wet mixture:
4 eggs, beaten (optional)
1⅓ cups milk
⅓ cup yogurt
⅓ cup water
1 teaspoon vanilla

amaranth

Hotcakes are popular in Mexico, even though they are not traditional. On the other hand, amaranth is traditional and has been in use since pre-Hispanic times. Amaranth is the highest protein grain, and has well balanced amino acids for nutritional requirements. These pancakes are light and fluffy, but they pack a lot of nourishment. You can mix enough dry ingredients for 2 or 3 batches, and store it in an airtight container in a cool place. This makes final preparation even faster.

Heat a pancake griddle or large, heavy skillet over medium heat. Mix the dry ingredients together, then mix the wet ingredients together. Combine the two mixtures with a minimum of movement to make a lumpy batter. Grease the griddle or skillet with a teaspoon of oil. Measure ½ cup of the batter, and place it on the hot griddle. Repeat until the space is filled with spreading pancakes. Cook until the bubbles that appear on the tops of the pancakes pop and stay open. Turn them over with a spatula, and cook for 1 more minute. Serve hot with butter and warmed maguey syrup, if you can get it, or maple syrup.

Per serving: Calories: 315, Protein: 16 gm., Fat: 8 gm., Carbohydrates: 43 gm.

Syrup Suggestions

Honey Orange Syrup

Try serving your pancakes with this honey-orange syrup when fresh oranges are abundant.

Mix all of the ingredients well.

Per ¼ cup: Calories: 178, Protein: 0 gm., Fat: 0 gm., Carbohydrates: 44 gm.

Makes ½ cup
Preparation time: 5 minutes

½ cup honey
2 tablespoons hot water
2 tablespoons fresh orange, lemon, or lime juice

Berry Syrup

You can make this delicious berry syrup in the summer when fresh berries are in season.

Boil the the berries and sugar for 1 hour, and strain.

Per ¼ cup: Calories: 185, Protein: 0 gm., Fat: 0 gm., Carbohydrates: 45 gm.

Makes 3 cups
Preparation time: 1 hour

1 pound berries (blackberries, blueberries, etc.)
½ pound sugar

Mario's Biscuits

Los Bisquets de Mario

Makes 1½-2 dozen biscuits
Preparation time: 20 minutes
Baking time: about 25 minutes

Mario learned to bake at his brother's side in La Casa del Pan in Tlalpan, Mexico City. His brother, Jeronimo, the head baker there, learned to make bread from me. Before that, they were construction workers on our house. Now, almost eight years down the line, they are an important part of that business (which is coordinated by our daughter, Amy, with the help of her husband, Rodrigo).

1¼ cups whole wheat flour
2 cups all purpose flour
¾ cup butter
2 tablespoons yogurt
½ teaspoon salt
6 tablespoons sugar
4 teaspoons baking powder
1½ teaspoons vanilla
1 cup milk

Preheat the oven to 350°F. Mix the flour with the butter, rolling it between your fingers to make a crumbly pea texture. Make a well in the middle of the flour mixture, and add the rest of the ingredients. Mix with your hands. Form into a ball and knead for 3 minutes. On a lightly floured board, using a lightly floured rolling pin, roll out to a thickness of ¾ inch. Cut with a cutter to the desired size, and bake on a lightly greased cookie sheet until they barely begin to brown.

Per biscuit: Calories: 143, Protein: 3 gm., Fat: 7 gm., Carbohydrates: 17 gm.

Flaky Pastry Dough

Masa Hojaldre

This is the dough we make for empanadas and niño envuelto (stuffed pastry roll). It also makes great pie crust, and it's delicious for quiche. It keeps well, refrigerated, for up to one week.

Place the flour in a large bowl. Make a well in the middle, and add the salt, water, and half of the butter. Mix to combine, then knead on a lightly floured board for 10 minutes, or until the dough is satiny smooth. Roll into a ball, and cut the ball into a 4-petalled flower shape. (See drawing 1.) Roll the "petals" and the center out. Work the chilled butter with your fists to flatten it out a bit, and place it in the center of the "flower." Enfold it within the four "petals," as shown in drawings 2 and 3, and seal it in by pinching the edges of the dough all around it. Roll out to a thickness of ¼ inch, in the shape of a rectangle, being careful not to break the dough. If the butter should start to come out, seal it in by pinching the dough over it. Mentally divide the rectangle into thirds, then fold the rectangle's side thirds over the middle third. Roll out into a rectangle ¼ inch thick, then repeat the folding over of the thirds. Roll out again, fold over again, cover, and refrigerate for at least three hours before using.

Per 24 pieces: Calories: 125, Protein: 3 gm., Fat: 3 gm., Carbohydrates: 19 gm.

Makes 2½ pounds of dough
Preparation time: 30 minutes

1½ pounds flour
1 teaspoon salt
1⅔ cups water
¼ pound unsalted butter, chilled

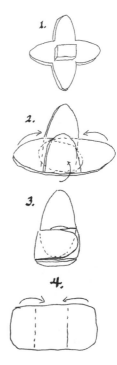

Empanadas

Empanada translates roughly as "breaded" and refers to filled pastries sold all over Mexico by street vendors, bakeries, and restaurants. Most people fry empanadas. We bake ours and everyone loves them that way. Try different fillings as you like. Oaxacan string cheese, or the equivalent, also makes a delicious filling.

Makes twelve 4-inch empanadas
Preparation time: 35 minutes
Cooking time: 25 minutes
Baking time: 35 minutes

Preheat the oven to 375°F. To form and bake the empanadas, roll out 1¾ lb. of pastry dough on a floured board to a thickness of ¼ inch. Use a saucer as a form to cut equal circles of dough. Form the leftover pieces into a ball, roll out, and cut until all the dough is used. Place a spoonful of filling on half of each circle of dough. Fold over the other half, and press the edges together with a fork. Place on a lightly greased cookie sheet, and bake for 35 minutes or until browned. They may also be partially baked (20 minutes) and then frozen between sheets of waxed paper.

Vegetable Filling

½ cup carrots, chopped
½ cup chayote, peeled and chopped (you may substitute green beans)
½ cup zucchini squash, chopped
½ cup onion, chopped
3 tablespoons cold pressed sesame or olive oil
½ teaspoon cumin
½ teaspoon chile powder
fine grain sea salt to taste
1 pound Flaky Pastry Dough (page 163), chilled

Steam the carrots and chayote for 3 minutes. Add the zucchini and steam for 2 more minutes. Sauté the onion in the oil over medium heat, stirring occasionally, for 5 minutes. Add the vegetables, cumin, chile powder, and sea salt, and remove from the heat. Allow to cool while you prepare the pastry dough.

Proceed forming and baking according to the instructions for Empanadas above.

Per serving (filling only): Calories: 52 , Protein: 1 gm., Fat: 2 gm., Carbohydrates: 6 gm.

Mushroom Filling
Relleno de Hongos

This filling is traditional in central and southern Mexico.

Sauté the mushrooms and scallions in the oil for 8 minutes. Add the herbs, chile, and salt, and sauté for another 2 minutes. Proceed forming and baking according to the recipe for Empanadas (page 164).

Per empanada (filling only): Calories: 54, Protein: 1 gm., Fat: 2 gm., Carbohydrates: 7 gm.

Makes twelve 4-inch empanadas
Preparation time: 15 minutes

1 pound mushrooms of any edible variety, chopped
3 scallions, chopped (greens included)
2 tablespoons sesame oil
2-3 leaves fresh epazote leaves, or 2 tablespoons fresh parsley
1 teaspoon fresh thyme, or ½ teaspoon dried thyme
pinch of ground pequín chile
½ teaspoon fine sea salt, or to taste
1 pound Flaky Pastry Dough (page 163), chilled

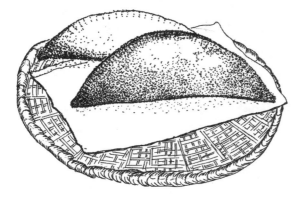

empanadas

Huitlacoche Filling
Relleno de Huitlacoche

Makes twelve 4-inch empanadas
Preparation time: 15 minutes

Huitlacoche is a black mushroom that grows on corn. It can be bought in cans in the Mexican specialty section of the supermarket. This filling, traditional in central Mexico, can be used either in baked empanadas or in griddle-cooked quesadillas.

3 tablespoons sunflower oil
½ medium onion, chopped
½ pound huitlacoche (if using canned, use three 4-ounce cans)
4-5 fresh epazote leaves, or 1 tablespoon fresh cilantro, chopped
½ teaspoon sea salt
1 pound Flaky Pastry Dough, chilled (page 163)

Heat the oil in a medium-sized skillet over medium heat. Sauté the onion until transparent, about 3-4 minutes. Add the huitlacoche and cook, stirring, for 8 minutes. Add the epazote leaves and salt, and continue to cook for another 2 minutes. Proceed forming and baking according to the recipe for Empanadas (page 164).

Per empanada (filling only): Calories: 79, Protein: 1 gm., Fat: 3 gm., Carbohydrates: 11 gm.

Squash Blossom Filling
Relleno de Flor de Calabaza

Here's a practical way to avoid being inundated with zucchini in August. Harvest the flowers and make squash blossom empanadas or quesadillas. This filling can be used for either.

Heat the oil over medium heat in an 8-inch skillet. Sauté the onion until transparent. Add the squash blossoms, chiles, and jalapeño, and continue to cook for 3 minutes. Add the marjoram and salt, stir to blend, and remove from heat. Proceed forming and baking according to the recipe for Empanadas (page 164).

Per empanada (filling only): Calories: 82, Protein: 2 gm., Fat: 2 gm., Carbohydrates: 11 gm.

Makes twelve 4-inch empanadas
Preparation time: 15 minutes

3 tablespoons olive oil
1 medium onion, thinly sliced
4 dozen squash blossoms
3 poblano chiles, seeded and finely chopped
1-4 fresh jalapeño chiles, chopped
pinch of marjoram
½ teaspoon sea salt, or to taste
1 pound Flaky Pastry Dough (page 163), chilled

Potato Filling
Relleno de Papa

Makes twelve 4-inch empanadas
Preparation time: 20 minutes

½ pound new potatoes, boiled
   until soft (about 15 minutes)
½ cup low-fat milk, plain yogurt,
   or water
3 tablespoons fresh parsley,
   finely chopped
freshly grated pepper
½ teaspoon sea salt, or to taste
¼ pound fresh white cheese or
   soy cheese, crumbled or grated
   (optional)
1 pound Flaky Pastry Dough
   (page 163), chilled

This filling is light and fluffy.

Using an electric mixer, beat the potatoes with half of the milk, adding the rest of the milk gradually as you continue to beat. Add the parsley, pepper, salt, and cheese, and mix well. Proceed forming and baking according to the recipe for Empanadas (page 164).

Per empanada (filling only): Calories: 40, Protein: 1 gm., Fat: 0 gm., Carbohydrates: 9 gm.

Saffron Potato Filling
Rellenos de Papa con Azafrán

If you have it, use cuesa, the root of the chayote, instead of the potato in this recipe. The saffron is Spanish in origin. This dish was adapted from a colonial pastry recipe.

Makes twelve 4-inch empanadas
Preparation time: 30 minutes

Drop the carrots, potatoes, and saffron into the boiling water, and boil for 5 minutes. Add the zucchini and boil, uncovered, until the carrots and potatoes are tender, about 5-10 minutes.

In a large nonstick skillet, heat the oil and slightly sauté the green onion. Add the jalapeño and cook for 3 more minutes, stirring occasionally with a wooden spoon. Drain the cooked vegetables and add to the skillet, reserving the cooking liquid.

In a separate small pan, simmer the saffron water until it is reduced to ½ cup. Continue to cook the vegetables over medium heat, stirring, until the potatoes begin to brown. Add the tomato and cook for 2 more minutes. Add the ½ cup saffron water, and cook, stirring, until the liquid is absorbed. Salt to taste. Proceed forming and baking according to the recipe for Empanadas (page 164).

Per empanada (filling only): Calories: 57, Protein: 1 gm., Fat: 2 gm., Carbohydrates: 8 gm.

½ cup carrots, peeled and diced
2½ cups potatoes or cuesa, peeled and diced
3 saffron threads
2 cups boiling water
½ cup zucchini, diced
2 tablespoons sunflower oil
¼ cup green onion, finely chopped
1 jalapeño chile, seeded and finely chopped
1 medium tomato, peeled, seeded, and chopped
1 teaspoon sea salt
1 pound Flaky Pastry Dough (page 163), chilled

Apple Empanadas

Empanadas de Manzana

Makes twelve 4-inch empanadas
Preparation time: 20 minutes
Baking time: 25 minutes

3 cups apples, peeled and finely
  chopped
1 tablespoon brown sugar
1-2 teaspoons ground cinnamon
½ cup raisins
½ cup pecans, chopped
1 tablespoon butter
1 tablespoon lime juice
1 pound Flaky Pastry Dough
  (page 163), chilled

There are many variations of apple empanadas in Mexico. I learned this recipe from my neighbor, Beatrice Uribe, who operates a small bakery in Mexico City called La Hogaza. They are baked, have a flaky crust, and are filled with finely chopped apples and nuts. They are spiced with cinnamon and fresh lime juice.

Combine all of the ingredients, except the pastry dough, and mix well. Preheat the oven to 375°F. On a lightly floured surface, role out the pastry dough in a rectangular shape, ⅛-inch thick. Cut into 12 equal-size rectangles. Place ⅓ cup of the filling in the middle of each rectangle. Fold the sides over the filling, and seal the edges together by pressing with the tines of a fork. Sprinkle the empanadas with a mixture of 2 tablespoons sugar and ½ teaspoon cinnamon. Place on an ungreased cookie sheet, and bake until golden brown, about 25 minutes.

Per empanada: Calories: 134, Protein: 2 gm., Fat: 4 gm., Carbohydrates: 22 gm.

Desserts

Postres

Custard

Flan

Serves 8
Preparation time: 20 minutes
Baking time: 40 minutes
Chilling time: 2 hours

1½ cups light brown sugar
4 cups milk
1 teaspoon vanilla extract
1 teaspoon almond extract
¼ teaspoon salt
4 eggs
½ teaspoon cornstarch

Flan was originally a Spanish dessert, but it is made throughout Mexico and is popular with everyone.

Preheat the oven to 350°F. Heat ¾ cup sugar in a heavy saucepan over medium heat, stirring constantly until the sugar dissolves and caramelizes. Pour into a 9-inch ovenproof baking ring, tilting it until the caramel covers the sides evenly. Put aside.

Heat the milk and the rest of the sugar in a medium saucepan until it boils, turn down the heat, and cook uncovered for 15 minutes. Remove from the heat and add the vanilla and almond extracts and salt.

Beat the eggs lightly with a wire whisk, then dissolve the cornstarch in a tablespoon of cold water, and add to the beaten eggs. Gradually add the warm milk and sugar to the egg mixture, stirring constantly. Pour this mixture into the caramel-coated baking ring. Place the ring in a round 12-inch cake pan or casserole, pour in an inch of hot water to the bottom of the outer container, and bake for approximately 40 minutes or until firm. Remove from the oven and allow to cool at room temperature before removing from the mold and refrigerating. Serve well chilled.

Per serving: Calories: 193, Protein: 8 gm., Fat: 5 gm., Carbohydrates: 31 gm.

Rice Pudding

Budin de Arroz

My kids always asked me for this dessert, which is of Spanish origin. It is served throughout Mexico and is nutritious and delicious!

Serves 6
Preparation time: 5 minutes
Cooking time: 30 minutes
Chilling time: 2 hours

Heat the rice, water, cinnamon, and salt to boiling, cover, and lower the heat. Cook for 20 minutes, then add the milk, sugar, raisins, and vanilla, stirring to combine. Cook for 10 minutes more and remove from heat. Allow to cool 15 minutes before serving, or refrigerate for two hours before serving.

Per serving: Calories: 306, Protein: 7 gm., Fat: 2 gm., Carbohydrates: 65 gm.

1 cup white rice
3 cups water
one 3-inch piece of stick cinnamon
⅛ teaspoon sea salt
4 cups milk
1 cup brown sugar, honey, or maguey syrup
½ cup raisins
1 teaspoon vanilla

Coconut Custard

Cocada

Serves 8
Preparation time: 30 minutes
Baking time: 30 minutes

1 medium coconut
1 cup coconut milk
1 cup milk
1 cup light brown sugar
3 eggs
1 teaspoon almond extract

This recipe is for coconut lovers. If you can't get fresh coconut, you may use packaged coconut instead, and either replace the coconut milk with water or use canned coconut milk. If you use the latter and it comes sweetened, eliminate or reduce the sugar accordingly. The results, however, will not be as outstanding as that achieved by using fresh coconut and coconut milk.

Open a hole in the coconut, and shake out the liquid into a bowl. Break the coconut open with a hammer. With a knife, cut and pry the white flesh away from the hull in chunks, and grate. Boil the grated coconut, coconut milk, milk, and brown sugar together for 15 minutes. Remove from the heat. Beat the eggs together with the almond extract, and add the coconut mixture gradually, stirring constantly. Preheat the oven to 325°F. Return to the heat and cook on low, stirring constantly, until the mixture thickens. Pour into a buttered, 9 x 9-inch baking pan, and bake until lightly browned, about 30 minutes. Serve cool, cut into 8 squares.

Per serving: Calories: 461, Protein: 7 gm., Fat: 35 gm., Carbohydrates: 29 gm.

Mamey Pudding

Budin de Mamey

Mamey is a fruit of the zapote family and is grown in the tropical regions of Mexico. It looks like a rough, dusty brown, thick-skinned, hand-sized football. Inside, it is a rich orange color and has exquisite flavor when ripe. It is difficult to select ripe ones, so in the marketplace, the vendors obligingly cut them open for their customers to see the color. If mamey fruit is unobtainable, substitute ripe mangos, blended and strained, for this exotic, aromatic dessert from the Gulf Coast.

Serves 20
Preparation time: 30 minutes
Chilling time: 2 hours

Boil the milk, cinnamon, and brown sugar, stirring occasionally until the mixture begins to thicken, about 20 minutes. Remove from the heat and gradually add the hot milk to the egg yolks. Return this mixture to the heat, and stir constantly, until the pudding thickens. Add the ground almonds and remove from the heat. Add the mamey pulp, mix, pour into a 2-quart dish, and refrigerate for at least 2 hours. Before serving, decorate with the chopped almonds and a mixture of cinnamon and sugar.

Per serving: Calories: 347, Protein: 10 gm., Fat: 18 gm., Carbohydrates: 35 gm.

3 quarts milk
2 sticks of cinnamon, about 5 inches long
3 cups brown sugar
9 egg yolks, slightly beaten
2½ cups almonds, peeled and ground
2 cups mamey pulp, blended with ¼ cup milk
½ cup chopped blanched almonds
2 teaspoons ground cinnamon
2 teaspoons sugar

Mexican Bread Fruit and Nut Pudding

Capirotada

Serves 6
Preparation time: 20 minutes
Baking time: 20 minutes

This typical dessert from northern Mexico is a delicious way to use old bread. Piloncillo is raw sugar that comes straight from the colonial sugar cane processing plants. It is formed into cones, which are stacked by fours and wrapped in the leaves of the sugar cane plant for shipping and sale.

20 slices whole wheat bolillo from 4 bolillos, or 10 slices whole grain bread (at least 2 days old)
½ cup butter
½ cups raisins
½ cup dates or dried apricots, chopped
½ cup peanuts or pecans, chopped
syrup:
1 cup piloncillo or or dark brown sugar
one 3-inch stick of cinnamon
4 cloves
1 cup water

Toast the bread lightly and spread with the butter. Prepare the syrup by boiling the brown sugar, cinnamon, and cloves in the water, uncovered, until it begins to thicken, about 10 minutes. Preheat the oven to 350°F. Dip each slice of bread in the syrup, and arrange in a layer in the bottom of a casserole. Cover with a layer of raisins, dates, and nuts. Repeat the layers until all the ingredients are used. Pour the remaining syrup over the capirotada, sprinkle with cinnamon sugar, cover, and bake for about 20 minutes. Serve warm.

Per serving: Calories: 703, Protein: 13 gm., Fat: 28 gm., Carbohydrates: 95 gm.

Orange Caramel Crepes

Crepes de Cajeta

Cajeta is caramelized milk, made by simmering goat's milk with sugar for several hours. It is found everywhere in Guanajuato, in many different flavors, shapes, and sizes, in roadside stands and sweet shops. Cajeta can be found in supermarkets all over Mexico and in many stores in the U.S., but in less variety.

Make the cajeta ahead of time, or buy it in the Mexican section of the supermarket. Dissolve the baking soda in water, and reserve. Combine the milk, sugar, and vanilla, and bring to a boil in a 2-quart saucepan. Reduce the heat until the milk is gently simmering, and gradually add the soda-water in a thin stream. Cook, without moving, for about 1½ hours, or until the milk has turned a light caramel color and will coat a wooden spoon.

The crepes can be made ahead of time and stored between waxed paper in the refrigerator.

To make the crepes, combine the egg, flour, and milk in a blender. Heat a crepe pan and melt about ¼ teaspoon of butter in it. Measure ⅛ cup batter into the pan, rotating the pan so that the batter covers the bottom evenly. Cook over medium heat until the bottom of the crepe is browned, and flip over onto a plate. Repeat.

To make the sauce, melt the butter in a small pan. Add the orange juice and cajeta, and heat for 5 minutes over medium heat, stirring. Add the rum and light with a match. Allow the alcohol to evaporate. Just before serving, form each crepe into a triangle by folding it in half and then in half again. Submerge in the sauce and arrange 2 on each plate. Cover with the rest of the sauce, and sprinkle with the pecans. Serve hot.

Serves 6
Preparation time: 10 minutes
Cooking time: (for the cajeta)
1½ hours
Cooking time: (for the crepes)
3 minutes each crepe

Cajeta:
¼ teaspoon baking soda
1 tablespoon water
1 quart goat's milk (or cow's milk)
1 cup sugar
1 teaspoon vanilla
crepes:
1 egg
½ cup flour
1½ cups milk
1 tablespoon melted butter for frying the crepes
Orange Cajeta Sauce:
2 tablespoons butter
½ cup orange juice
1 cup cajeta
1 tablespoon rum
½ cup chopped pecans

Per serving: Calories: 435, Protein: 11 gm., Fat: 19 gm., Carbohydrates: 51 gm.

San Cristobal Peach Pie

Serves 6 to 8
Preparation time: 30 minutes
Baking time: 35 to 40 minutes

4 cups sliced peaches
1 tablespoon lime juice
2 cups sliced mangos
2 teaspoons cinnamon
1 teaspoon allspice
½ cup honey
1 tablespoon butter
1 double Pie Crust (page 179)

Peach season in the highlands of Chiapas is marked by Indian kids selling peaches by the pail along the highways, flagging down the travellers and insisting that they buy. You always buy more than you planned.

Preheat the oven to 400°F. Gently combine the peaches, lime juice, mangos, cinnamon, allspice, honey, and butter. Line a 10-inch pie pan with half of the pie crust, trim it around the edge, and fill with the fruit mixture. Place the other half of the crust over the pie, cut to fit, and pinch the edges together. Cut slits in the top crust to allow steam to escape, and sprinkle with 1 teaspoon brown sugar, if desired. Bake for 10 minutes at 400°F. Reduce the temperature to 350°F and bake another 25 to 30 minutes or until golden brown.

Per serving: Calories: 448, Protein: 5 gm., Fat: 19 gm., Carbohydrates: 60 gm.

Pie Crust

The secret to successful pie crust is to use well-chilled butter and to work quickly, before the dough warms up and becomes sticky.

Mix the flours and cut in the butter with a pastry cutter or two knives until the butter looks like flour-coated peas. Mix in the ice water and collect the dough into a ball. Cut into two equal parts, and form into balls. Place one in the refrigerator. Place the other ball on a board lightly floured with whole wheat flour. (If the dough is no longer cold, it is better to chill it in the refrigerator for ½ hour before rolling out.)

With a lightly floured rolling pin, roll out the dough, working from the center out to the edges, to preserve the round shape. Use more dusting flour lightly, as required to keep the dough from sticking to the rolling pin or to the board. When the dough is slightly larger than the pie pan, loosen it gently from the counter with a spatula, and fold it in half, then fold it in half again and place in one quarter of the pan. Unfold, cut away the excess, and it is ready to be filled. Follow the same procedure for rolling out the top crust.

Per serving: Calories: 243, Protein: 3 gm., Fat: 16 gm., Carbohydrates: 21 gm.

Makes two 10-inch pie crusts
(8 servings)
Preparation time: 20 minutes

1 cup unbleached flour
1 cup whole wheat flour
⅔ cup chilled butter
6 tablespoons ice water

Grandmother Crocker's Persimmon Pudding

Makes 12 squares
Preparation time: 15 minutes
Baking time: 25 to 30 minutes

½ cup dates, chopped
½ cup raisins
½ cup walnuts or pecans, chopped
1 cup flour
1 teaspoon cinnamon
½ teaspoon baking soda
1 cup persimmon pulp
1 cup sugar
pinch of salt
½ cup milk
¼ cup butter
½ teaspoon lemon juice
1 teaspoon vanilla
hard sauce:
¼ cup butter, at room temperature
1 cup confectioner's sugar
1 egg yolk, well beaten
½ cup cream

This was the most delicious dessert I ever tried at my grandmother's house in southern California, where persimmons are as plentiful as they are in Mexico.

Preheat the oven to 350°F. Mix the dates, raisins, and nuts, and dust with a mixture of the flour, cinnamon, and baking soda. Add the persimmon pulp, sugar, and salt. Scald the milk and add the butter. Cool and add to the fruit mixture, along with the lemon juice and vanilla. Mix well and bake in a 9 x 12-inch pan until done, about 25 or 30 minutes.

While the pudding is baking, prepare the hard sauce by creaming the butter with an electric mixer. Add the confectioner's sugar gradually, and continue beating until smooth. Add 1 well-beaten egg yolk and then the cream. Beat 2 more minutes and refrigerate for 2 hours before serving. Serve the pudding cooled with the chilled hard sauce on top.

Per square: Calories: 342, Protein: 3 gm., Fat: 13 gm., Carbohydrates: 50 gm.

Mamey Mousse

The mamey is part of the zapote family, and its seeds are prized for the oil they yield. The Indian women of Oaxaca go to great effort to expell it to put on their hair, which makes it grow thick and luxuriously. To select ripe fruit, you must cut through the rough skin to see the color inside. Use only fruits with deep orange color and a good flavor.

Combine the water and sugar in a small saucepan. Bring to a boil and allow to simmer until a syrup is formed, about 10 minutes. Remove from the heat. Beat the egg whites until stiff but not dry. Add the warm syrup to them, while still beating. Fold the mamey purée into the beaten whites. In another bowl, whip the cream until thick, adding the confectioner's sugar gradually. Fold the cream into the mamey-egg white mixture. Pour into dessert dishes and refrigerate for at least 2 hours before serving.

Per serving: Calories: 287, Protein: 3 gm., Fat: 10 gm., Carbohydrates: 45 gm.

Serves 6-8
Preparation time: 20 minutes
Chilling time: 2 hours

1 cup water
1 cup sugar
4 egg whites
3 mamey fruits, peeled and mashed with a potato masher
1 cup whipping cream
¼ cup confectioner's sugar, sifted

Apple-Maguey Ring

Makes one 10-inch ring, (serves 8)
Preparation time: 15 minutes
Baking time: 45 minutes

This recipe uses maguey syrup, the product made by boiling down the nectar extracted from the heart of the maguey cactus. It was made by the Aztecs, who used it for curing colds, sore throats, and stomach ailments. It is not easy to find outside of Mexico, but some health food stores and Mexican specialty stores might be willing to order it from La Casa Ecologica de Teotihuacan, in San Juan Teotihuacan, Mexico. It is now also available from La Granja Organica, located in the Parque Ecológico Loreto y Peña Pobre, Tlalpan, Mexico City.

2 eggs
1 cup maguey syrup, brown
  sugar, honey, or molasses
1 cup safflower oil
3½ cups apples, chopped
1 teaspoon vanilla extract
¼ teaspoon salt
¼ teaspoon baking soda
3 cups whole wheat flour
1 teaspoon cinnamon
1 cup pecans, chopped

Preheat the oven to 350°F. With a blender or mixer, beat the eggs together with the maguey syrup and oil, and pour into a mixing bowl. Add the apples and vanilla. Combine the salt, baking soda, flour, and cinnamon, and stir into the apple mixture. Add the pecans and mix lightly. Pour into a greased 10-inch ring, and bake until firm, about 45 minutes.

Per serving: Calories: 684, Protein: 7 gm., Fat: 35 gm., Carbohydrates: 80 gm.

Variation: *Mango Ring*
Follow the recipe for Apple-Maguey Ring, but substitute mangos for apples.

Mangos with Blackberry Sauce

Mangoes con Salsa de Mora

Serves 4
Preparation time: 10 minutes

Blend the blackberries with the sugar, lime juice, and water. Strain into a cup. Arrange the mango slices on individual dessert plates, and cover with the blackberry sauce.

Per serving: Calories: 199, Protein: 1 gm., Fat: 0 gm., Carbohydrates: 47 gm.

1 cup blackberries
¼ cup sugar
juice of ½ lime
½ cup water
4 mangoes, peeled and sliced

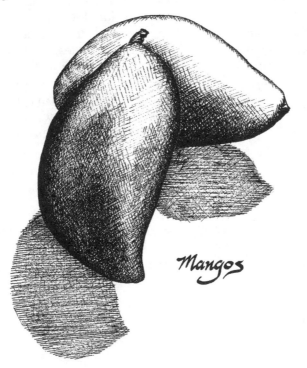

Mangos

Banana Flambé

Serves 6
Preparation time: 5 minutes
Baking time: 10 minutes

2 tablespoons brown sugar
1 teaspoon cinnamon
2 tablespoons butter
6 ripe bananas, peeled and sliced in half, lengthwise
3 tablespoons dark Caribbean rum, or 1 tablespoon lime juice + 2 tablespoons orange juice
3 tablespoons sliced almonds (optional)

Throughout tropical Mexico, a large variety of bananas are cultivated, ranging from the finger-sized dominicos to the fat red, guineos and the large plantains used for cooking. For this recipe any kind will do, as long as they are ripe.

Mix the brown sugar and cinnamon. Preheat the oven to 400°F. Grease a 9 x 12-inch ovenproof dish with butter, and sprinkle with half the cinnamon-sugar mix. Arrange the bananas in the dish with the cut side down. Sprinkle with the rest of the cinnamon-sugar mix, and dot with butter. Bake about 10 minutes, or until the bananas are well cooked. Remove from the oven, sprinkle with the rum, and ignite. If you use the citrus juice, ladle some over each banana on the serving plates. Sprinkle with the almonds. Serve hot, accompanied with vanilla ice cream and Spiced Pot Coffee (page 193).

Per serving: Calories: 191, Protein: 1 gm., Fat: 4 gm., Carbohydrates: 33 gm

Mexican-Style French Toast

Torrejas

This recipe has been traditional in the city of Puebla since colonial times. It's a delicious way to utilize baguettes or other bread when they're more than a day old.

Bring the milk, brown sugar, and cinnamon to a simmer, and remove from the heat. When cooled, pour over the bread slices, and allow to stand. Prepare the syrup by boiling the water, brown sugar, and cinnamon for 5 minutes. Remove from the heat. Add the orange rind and vanilla. Keep this syrup warm on the back of the stove while you prepare the toast.

Heat the oil and butter together in a skillet. Take a slice of bread from the milk mixture, dip it in the beaten eggs, coating both sides, and place in the skillet. Repeat with the other slices of bread, until the skillet is full. Fry until brown, turning to brown both sides. Remove to a warm plate. Keep the first pieces warm in the oven while the rest are frying. Add more oil and butter to the skillet if necessary. When all the slices of bread are browned, serve 2 on each plate with the warm syrup poured over the top.

Per serving: Calories: 626, Protein: 12 gm., Fat: 16 gm., Carbohydrates: 107 gm.

Serves 6
Preparation time: 25 minutes
Cooking time: 25 minutes

2 cups milk
⅓ cup dark brown sugar
one 3-inch piece of stick
   cinnamon
12 thick slices baguette, bolillo,
   or other bread
2 tablespoons oil
3 tablespoons butter
3 eggs, beaten
syrup:
2 cups water
2 cups raw or dark brown sugar
one 3-inch piece of stick
   cinnamon
1 teaspoon grated orange rind
1 teaspoon vanilla

Amaranth Cookies

Galletas de Amaranto

Makes 48 cookies
Preparation time: 10 minutes
Baking time: 20 minutes

1 teaspoon finely ground sea salt
½ pound (2¼ cups) amaranth
  flour
½ pound (1¾ cups) whole wheat
pastry
flour
1 pound amaranth cereal (the
  puffed amaranth seed)
2 tablespoons baking powder
1 cup milk
5 eggs, beaten
⅓ pound (⅔ cup) butter, melted
½ pound (1½ cups) sunflower
seeds, hulled
1¼ cups maguey syrup, or
  2 cups brown sugar, densely
  packed

Amaranth is native to Mexico. It is a tiny seed which is very high in protein (once suppling the indigenous population with a large portion of its protein) and is mild in flavor. If toasted to make it inflate, it makes a nice cereal, served with milk and honey. These cookies are an invention of one of my bread making students.

Preheat the oven to 350°F. Combine all the dry ingredients. Separately blend the wet ingredients. Combine the two mixtures and form into 1½-inch balls. Arrange on lightly greased cookie sheets, and bake for about 20 minutes, or until the cookies begin to brown on the bottom.

Per cookie: Calories: 157, Protein: 4 gm., Fat: 6 gm., Carbohydrates: 21 gm.

Ginger Cookies

Galletas de Jenjibre

Fresh gingerroot is the secret of these fragrant cookies. They keep well in a cookie jar or tin and make a special gift to someone special anytime.

Combine the 2 flours, baking soda, and salt. Beat the butter and add the eggs one at a time. Add the sugars and then the flour mixture, combining well after each addition. Add the ginger, cinnamon, cloves, allspice, lime rind, orange rind, and yogurt, and stir until well mixed. Preheat the oven to 375°F. Form the dough into teaspoon-sized balls, and arrange on a lightly greased sheet. Bake for 10 minutes until the cookies barely begin to brown.

Per cookie: Calories: 86, Protein: 1 gm., Fat: 3 gm., Carbohydrates: 12 gm.

Makes 5 dozen cookies
Preparation time: 15 minutes
Baking time: 10 minutes

2½ cups whole wheat flour
2½ cups white flour
1¼ teaspoons baking soda
½ teaspoon salt
1 cup butter
2 eggs, beaten
1 cup white sugar
1 cup dark brown sugar
4 teaspoons ground ginger
1 teaspoon ground cinnamon
½ teaspoon ground cloves
½ teaspoon ground allspice
1 teaspoon grated lime or lemon rind
1 teaspoon grated orange rind
3 tablespoons yogurt

Orange-Ring Cookies

Roscas de Naranja

Makes about 24 cookies
Preparation time: 20 minutes
Baking time: 10 minutes

4 cups white flour, sifted first
1 teaspoon baking powder
1 cup butter
1 cup light brown sugar
¾ cup yogurt
grated rind of two oranges
light brown sugar for covering

These easy-to-make cookies have an aroma of orange and a taste of butter.

Sift the flour with the baking powder. Beat the butter until creamy. Gradually add the sugar while continuing to beat, and then the yogurt. Gradually add the flour, baking powder, and orange rind, and continue beating until the dough is satin-smooth (about 2 minutes with an electric beater). Preheat the oven to 350°F.

Sprinkle a counter or tabletop lightly with flour, and roll out the dough with a rolling pin to a thickness of ¼-inch. Cut out each cookie with the top of a water glass or a 2-inch cookie cutter. Cut out the center by pressing the mouth of a soda bottle into the middle of each cookie. Bake on a lightly floured cookie sheet until the cookies barely begin to brown, about 10 minutes. Cool for 5 minutes, then bury them in light brown sugar before arranging them on a serving dish.

Per cookie: Calories: 166, Protein: 2 gm., Fat: 8 gm., Carbohydrates: 21 gm.

Drinks

Bebidas

Atole

Atole is a hot, pre-Colombian beverage made with corn masa and water. It is sweetened with piloncillo (raw sugar) and flavored with fruit, chocolate, chile, vanilla or nuts. It is widely popular in Mexico, where is served with tamales. Following are three different recipes, which can form the basis for numerous variations. Atole is especially recommended for nursing mothers and young children.

Pineapple Atole
Piña Atole

Serves 6
Preparation time: 25 minutes

¼ pound masa for tortillas
6 cups water
2 cups fresh pineapple, coarsely chopped
1 cup (¼ pound) piloncillo or dark brown sugar
2 cups fresh pineapple, finely chopped

Dissolve the masa in 4 cups water, and allow to stand 10 minutes. Meanwhile, blend 2 cups pineapple with 1 cup water. Strain through a sieve and reserve the juice. In a 2-quart saucepan, heat the masa water, the piloncillo, the pineapple juice, and 1 cup water, stirring continuously until the mixture begins to thicken, about 10 minutes. Serve hot.

Per serving: Calories: 203, Protein: 1 gm., Fat: 0 gm., Carbohydrates: 49 gm.

Variations: *Fruit Atole—Vanilla Atole*
This recipe can be employed to make atole with strawberries, guavas, raspberries, blackberries, mangos, or other suitable fruit. To make vanilla atole, eliminate the fruit, and add 2 teaspoons vanilla extract at the end of the cooking.

Amaranth Atole

Amaranto Atole

Amaranth is high in protein and makes a very nourishing atole. It has a mild, sweet, agreeable flavor and a subtle aroma. This recipe is from the state of Morelos. It was given to me by the amaranth grower himself, my friend Guillermo Castillo.

Serves 6
Preparation time: 15 minutes

In a 2-quart saucepan, place the amaranth flour and gradually add the water, stirring constantly to blend. Heat over medium heat, stirring until thickened. Remove from the heat, add the cinnamon stick, and stir in the honey. Serve hot.

¾ cup amaranth flour
6 cups water (or milk)
one 3-inch stick of cinnamon
¾ cup honey or brown sugar

Per serving: Calories: 163, Protein: 1 gm., Fat: 0 gm., Carbohydrates: 39 gm.

Almond Atole

Almendra Atole

Serves 6
Preparation time: 25 minutes

Dissolve the masa in 6 cups of water. Blend the almonds, ½ cup at a time. Add the almonds to the masa water, together with the piloncillo. Heat over medium heat, stirring continuously, until thickened. Serve hot.

¼ pound tortilla masa
6 cups water
1 cup almonds, blanched and peeled
1 cup piloncillo or brown sugar

Per serving: Calories: 301, Protein: 5 gm., Fat: 12 gm., Carbohydrates: 43 gm.

Amy's Oatmeal Horchata

Horchata de Avena

Serves 6
Preparation time: 40 minutes

1 cup rolled oats
1 cup milk
1 teaspoon ground cinnamon
1 teaspoon vanilla
½ cup sugar
4 cups water

This delicious horchata is very popular at Amy's La Casa del Pan in Mexico City.

Combine the oats, milk cinnamon, vanilla, and sugar in a blender, and blend until smooth. Pour into a 6-cup pitcher, chill for ½ hour, stir, and serve.

Per serving: Calories: 199, Protein: 6 gm., Fat: 3 gm., Carbohydrates: 39 gm.

Rice Horchata

Horchata de Arroz

Serves 6
Preparation time: 2¼ hours
(includes 2 hours for soaking)

2 cups rice
6 cups water
2 tablespoons blanched almonds
½ teaspoon cinnamon
⅓ cup sugar

This cool, Spanish drink is served throughout Mexico.

Soak the rice in the water for 2 hours. Grind in a blender with the almonds, and strain. Add the cinnamon and sugar, and chill for 1 hour before serving.

Per serving: Calories: 132, Protein: 3 gm., Fat: 0 gm., Carbohydrates: 29 gm.

Spiced Pot Coffee

Cafe de Olla

This coffee is so good, cooked slowly in an earthenware pot, and served with tamales for a special brunch.

Serves 8
Preparation time: 20 minutes

Bring the water to a boil in the pot. Lower the heat to a minimum, and add the brown sugar, cinnamon, cloves, and orange peel. Simmer for 15 minutes. Remove from the heat, and add the coffee. Cover, and allow to brew for 5 minutes. Add ½ cup cold water to settle the coffee grounds. Pour through a fine sieve into a serving pitcher, and serve.

Per serving: Calories: 58, Protein: 0 gm., Fat: 0 gm., Carbohydrates: 14 gm.

earthenware pot, if possible
2 quarts water
¼ pound dark brown sugar
two 3-inch sticks of cinnamon
3 whole cloves
peel of ½ small orange
¾ cup freshly ground, roasted coffee

Oaxacan Hot Chocolate Atole

Champurrado de Oaxaca

Serves 8-12
Preparation time: 1 hour

- ½ pound masa harina
- 3 quarts water
- ½ cup dark brown sugar or piloncillo
- one 3-inch stick of cinnamon
- ½ pound Mexican chocolate

This is a hot chocolate drink, an atole from Oaxaca. The recipe is traditional.

Dissolve the masa harina in 1 quart of the water, and allow to stand for 15 minutes. Strain and put it in a 4-quart saucepan with the rest of the water, brown sugar, and cinnamon. Bring to a boil and reduce the heat to a simmer. Cook, stirring, for 10 minutes. Add the chocolate and cook until it melts, stirring continuously. Serve hot.

Per serving: Calories: 264, Protein: 5 gm., Fat: 17 gm., Carbohydrates: 25 gm.

Lemonade with Chia

Agua de Chia con Limon

Serves 5
Preparation time: 3 minutes

- ¼ cup chía seeds
- ¼ cup freshly squeezed lime or lemon juice
- ¼ cup light brown sugar
- 5 cups water

Chía seeds grow in the northern Mexican desert. It is eaten to promote health and stamina. They are high in protein.

In two batches, combine all of the ingredients in a blender, and blend well. Serve chilled, stirring to mix the chía, which settles quickly.

Per serving: Calories: 30, Protein: 0 gm., Fat: 0 gm., Carbohydrates: 8 gm.

Cantaloupe Cooler

Horchata de Melon

Serves 6
Preparation time: 5 minutes
Chilling time: 2 hours

Blend or process the cantaloupe in 3 batches with ¼ cup water each time. Blend or process the seeds with ¼ cup water. Add the rest of the water, lime juice, and honey, and refrigerate for 2 hours. Strain the seeds through a wire mesh strainer.

Per serving: Calories: 32, Protein: 1 gm., Fat: 0 gm., Carbohydrates: 7 gm.

1 medium cantaloupe, cut into quarters and peeled
3 cups water
the seeds of the melon
1 tablespoon lime juice
¼ cup honey (optional)

Cold Fruit Punch

Ponche de Fruta Fresca

This recipe is sweet without any sugar, if the fruit is ripe.

Blend or process the pineapple in two batches with ½ cup of the water for each batch, and strain. Blend or process the rest of the fruit in batches with a little of the water for each batch, and strain. Combine all of the juice, and chill before serving.

Per serving: Calories: 119, Protein: 1 gm., Fat: 0 gm., Carbohydrates: 27 gm.

Serves 8
Preparation time: 15 minutes

3 cups pineapple, peeled and cut in chunks
2 cups red papaya, peeled and cut in chunks
2 cups washed guavas
4 cups freshly squeezed orange juice
2 cups water or carbonated spring water

Hot Guava Fruit Punch

Ponche Caliente de Guayaba

Serves 20
Preparation time: 30 minutes
Cooking time: 30 minutes

2 pounds guavas, chopped
2 pounds (5⅓ cups) apples,
  chopped
½ pound (1¾ cups) whole, pitted
  prunes
½ pound (1½ cups) raisins
4 ounces stick cinnamon
2 tablespoons whole allspice
1 teaspoon cloves
6 quarts water
3 cones of piloncillo, or
  1 pound (2 cups) brown sugar
¼ pound dried hibiscus
  (Jamaica) flowers

This punch is inspired by the guava-based fruit punch prepared in San Cristobal de Las Casas (which I like to call San Cristobal de Las Fiestas, since the town is wild about fiestas). There is cause for a fiesta every day of the year in some part of the town. You will hear fireworks sounding off at dawn and marimbas or mariachis playing dance music all night long. Really!

Combine all the ingredients in a 2-gallon pot, cover, and bring to a boil. Remove the lid, and boil for 30 minutes. Serve hot in cups with saucers and spoons for eating the fruit. In San Cristobal this is served with "posh," the local bootleg rum.

Per serving: Calories: 207, Protein: 1 gm., Fat: 0 gm., Carbohydrates: 49 gm.

Tascalate

This drink is very popular in the southern state of Chiapas, where it has been made since prehispanic times. Cacahuazintle, or hominy corn, is traditionally used. This is the same corn used for making pozole. In this recipe I have substituted cornmeal for the hominy.

Combine all the ingredients and store in a glass container. To prepare the tascalate, mix 2 heaping tablespoons of the mixture with 1 cup cold water or milk, and blend.

Per serving: Calories: 94, Protein: 2 gm., Fat: 0 gm., Carbohydrates: 19 gm.

Serves 24
Preparation time: 5 minutes

2 cups cornmeal
¾ cup cocoa
2 tortillas, toasted in a dry skillet until crisp, and then ground with a rolling pin
2 teaspoons achiote, ground
1 teaspoon cinnamon
1½ cups light brown sugar, or to taste

Papaya Orange Shake

Licuado de Papaya con Naranja

Serves 4
Preparation time: 5 minutes

2 cups fresh papaya
3 cups freshly squeezed orange juice
¼ cup honey (optional)

Blend the papaya with the 1 cup of the juice and the honey. Gradually add the rest of the juice. Serve at once.

Per serving: Calories: 96, Protein: 1 gm., Fat: 0 gm., Carbohydrates: 22 gm.

Papaya

Pineapple Parsley Drink

Licuado de Piña con Perejil

Serves 4
Preparation time: 5 minutes

2 cups fresh pineapple
½ cup fresh parsley, washed and coarsely chopped
¼ cup light brown sugar (optional)
3 cups water

A surprisingly delicious combination and highly nutritious, as well.

In a blender, combine the pineapple, parsley, sugar, and 2 cups water, and blend until smooth. Add the rest of the water, mix, and serve.

Per serving: Calories: 41, Protein: 0 gm., Fat: 0 gm., Carbohydrates: 9 gm.

Jamaica Iced Tea

Jamaica tea is made from dried hibiscus flowers. They make a delicious tea that is high in vitamin C.

Add the flowers to the boiling water, turn off the heat, cover, and let stand for 1 hour, Strain, add the lime juice and sweetener, and refrigerate until cold.

Per serving: Calories: 10, Protein: 0 gm., Fat: 0 gm., Carbohydrates: 2 gm.

Serve 6-8
Preparation time: 2 hours

1½ cups dried Jamaica (hibiscus) flowers
2 quarts boiling water
juice of two limes
sweetener (optional)

Index

Ethnic Favorites from Book Publishing Company

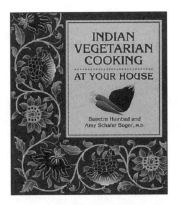

Indian Vegetarian
Cooking at Your House
$12.95

From A Traditional
Greek Kitchen
$12.95

From the
Tables of Lebanon
$12.95

Delicious Jamaica
$11.95

Nonna's Italian Kitchen
$14.95

Flavors of the Southwest
$12.95

Ask your local book or health food store to carry these titles, or you
may order directly from: Book Publishing Company
                             P.O. Box 99
                             Summertown, TN 38483
                             1-800-695-2241
Please add $2.50 per book for shipping and handling.